W9-ATQ-390

THE UNITED STATES AND SPAIN:

An Interpretation

THE UNITED STATES AND SPAIN:

An Interpretation

BY

CARLTON J. H. HAYES

Former American Ambassador to Spain

GREENWOOD PRESS, PUBLISHERS
WESTPORT, CONNECTICUT

Reprinted by permission
of Sheed & Ward, Inc., Publishers

First Greenwood Reprinting 1970

SBN 8371-2805-6

PRINTED IN UNITED STATES OF AMERICA

CONTENTS

NOTE

The following chapters are an expanded version of the Fenwick Lectures which the author was privileged to deliver in 1951 at the College of the Holy Cross, Worcester, Massachusetts.

Two reference maps have been added: *English and Hispanic Areas of the Atlantic Community* on page 17, and *Spain* on page 133. The latter is derived, with the kind permission of the Bruce Publishing Company, from a sketch map in Mr. Richard Pattee's recent volume.

THE UNITED STATES AND SPAIN:

An Interpretation

I.

Fellow Members of the Atlantic Community

1.

Today America as a whole is almost half English in speech and tradition and almost half Spanish (or Portuguese). Spanish settlement here came first. It followed immediately the famous transatlantic voyage of Christopher Columbus, over four and a half centuries ago; and it marked the beginning of a revolutionary expansion of the area of Western Christian civilization. Hitherto, this civilization had centered in the Mediterranean and been confined to countries north of it in central and western Europe. Henceforth it would center in the Atlantic and stretch out over the continents on both sides of it. What had been a Mediterranean or strictly European community of nations would become an Atlantic Community.

Columbus's exploit needs no recounting or embellishment. It was one of the great achievements in human history, and it was a Spanish achievement. I know, of course, that Columbus himself, like many other experienced sea captains of his time, was Italian by birth, and I have no doubt that long before him Norse sailors had visited coasts of North America, and that, in ages much farther back, Mongoloid and Polynesian peoples had found their way across Bering Strait or the Pacific and provided ancestry for American Indians. Yet the really significant event for us is the Europeanization of America—the creation of the Atlantic Community—and this started under Spanish auspices. Columbus was in the service of Spain. He was encouraged by Spanish friars and Spanish university professors. He was financed and patronized by Queen Isabella of Castile. His ships were built in Spain and manned by Spaniards. It was the royal standard of Spain which he raised on his first landing in America, and it was Spaniards whom he left as the first permanent settlers of the Old World in the New. Columbus died a Spaniard, and his collateral descendants are still grandees of Spain.

All this was fully recognized, and grateful homage paid to it, four centuries later in the United States. The Chicago World's Fair of 1893 (originally planned for 1892) was a grandiose tribute to Columbus and to Spain. A Spanish Infanta was the central guest of honor, and a special issue of our postage stamps commemorated not only Columbus but Queen Isabella and the Friars of La Rabida. October twelfth, Columbus Day, was then observed as an essentially Spanish holiday, no less in the United States than in Spain and Spanish America. A bit strange it is that fifty years later our observance of Columbus Day has taken on an Italian complexion.

The effective discovery and early settlement of America occurred at a time when western and central Europe was relatively a unit in manners and ideas. It was a time when Italy and Germany, the Low Countries and Scandinavia, France and Portugal, England and Spain alike professed the same Catholic Christian religion, and when all those countries were sharing in the transition from middle ages to renaissance. Everywhere there still survived medieval ways of living and working and traveling and at least the forms of medieval government—the charters of local and personal liberty, and the limitations on monarchy by representation of various social classes in parliament, estates, or cortes. Everywhere, too, the semi-pagan renaissance was permeating the upper and literate classes and ushering in an age of shameless self-seeking and lusty adventure, the age of Ferdinand and Isabella in Spain and the early Tudors in England. It was also an age of "merchant adventurers" in England, of "free knights" in Germany, and of Spanish conquistadores—a Cortez, a Pizarro, and many another.

The conquest of more than half of all America, including its hottest coasts and most rugged interior, was accomplished by the conquistadores within an astonishingly short time after Columbus's initial voyage. They were drawn from many walks of life, frequently from very lowly, but in their courage, their self-esteem, and their greed for glory as well as for wealth, they resembled the knights described over two centuries previously by Alfonso the Wise in his famous Code of Laws. "Knights," that Spanish King had explained, should be chosen "from the hunters of the hills, who are men who can suffer much hardship, and carpenters and smiths and stonecutters, for they are used to striking hard and are stronghanded. And also from the butchers, because they are used to killing live things and to spill blood . . . . They all should be tough, strong, and swift." [1]

The breed of conquistadores was not peculiar to Spain and Spanish America. The line of English adventurers from Hawkins and Drake to Captain Cook were of the same kidney and might properly be described as conquistadores of the sea. Nor is the famed frontiersman of English-speaking America

---

[1] Quoted by Salvador de Madariaga in his *Fall of the Spanish American Empire,* p. 13.

without some spiritual affinity to the Spanish conquistador. Such types have been a common and distinguishing feature of Western civilization and of the whole Atlantic Community. The Spanish variety was perhaps a bit more colorful, and at any rate it was ahead of any other in seizing upon the "New World" as a challenging, limitless field for its exertions.

For Spain had a head start of more than a century over any other European country in the conquest, colonization, and exploitation of America.[1] During that period, thanks to the joint and at times rival efforts of Spanish conquistadores and Spanish friars and priests and to the constant fostering care of the Spanish crown, the bulk of South America and the whole of the Caribbean area were infused with Western civilization and made into a Spanish preserve—a huge transatlantic New Spain.

2.

The whole of North America, on top of South America and the Caribbean area, proved too extensive for Spanish penetration and occupation in the sixteenth

[1] Except, of course, in Brazil, where Portugal made settlements. Portugal, however, was joined to the Spanish crown from 1580 to 1641, and it was not until 1750 that approximately the present-day boundaries were definitely drawn between Spanish America and Portuguese Brazil.

century. Spanish resources of men and means were limited, after all, and they did not suffice for such farflung oversea enterprise, immensely complicated as this became by simultaneous conflicts of Spain with a wide variety of European rivals, including Turkey, Portugal, Holland, France, and England. Although Spain successfully repelled the Turks in the Mediterranean and preserved the bulk of what she actually held across the Atlantic, she could not prevent the Dutch, the French, or the English from securing footholds in North America and on minor Caribbean islands. The upshot was that a hundred and thirty years after Columbus's initial voyage, "New Spain" was confronted in America by a "New England," a "New France," and a "New Netherlands."

In the course of the next two centuries, as we all know, New Netherlands and New France, except for small remnants and romantic memories, passed out of existence and were incorporated in the English-speaking domain. By the middle of the nineteenth century, this domain, through the Continental expansion of the United States and Canada, covered most of North America. Since then, America as a whole has represented a definitely tripartite division; cultural boundaries have remained constant and clearly marked between English America, Spanish America, and Portuguese America.

These divisions, nevertheless, must not blind us to perception of the much more important, and indeed fundamental, fact that all America, whether Spanish, English, or Portuguese, is a frontier of Europe, and a sharer with Europe in a common Western civilization. Alike in the cases of Spain and Portugal, and of England, and likewise of France and Holland, there was a transplanting from Europe to America—a transplanting of population, language, religion, education, manners and customs. Consequently, from Buenos Aires and Valparaiso, up through Rio and Lima and Mexico City, to Williamsburg and New York, Boston and Quebec, the prevailing civilization has been unmistakably West European, and the cultural variations on the American side of the Atlantic have been chiefly derived from those on the European side.

Of course, Americans of European stock have been affected by peculiar conditions of frontier life. They have had to accustom themselves to a new and strange physical environment and adapt it to their use. They have had to clear virgin forests, build towns, and develop agriculture and industry afresh. Also unlike their kinsmen who remained in Europe, they have had to cope with significant race problems arising from the presence of indigenous Indians and the importation of African Negroes. But all these conditions have been peculiar to America as a whole, and not to any one European nationality within it. Spaniards and Portuguese, as well as Englishmen, have been frontiersmen. Englishmen, as well as Spaniards and Portuguese, have conquered Indians and enslaved Negroes.

Between America and Western Europe, commercial ties have long been intimate. For four centuries Europe has drawn upon America for raw materials, and America upon Europe for manufactured goods. The Atlantic is the most traveled of all oceans, the veritable inland sea of an economic as well as cultural community. Though the economic and commercial ties were originally knit by mercantilist policies aimed at exploiting American colonies for the exclusive benefit of the several mother-countries in Europe, those ties have actually been interwoven and strengthened during the past century and a half by the severance of political bonds between Europe and America and the accompanying breakdown of nationalistic trade monopolies. The freer it is, the more naturally does commercial intercourse draw together the whole Atlantic Community, and the more clearly does it indicate the interdependence of America and Europe.

Transatlantic commerce has been not only in goods, but in ideas, especially in political ideas and in institutions enshrining them. No doubt America has provided Europe with inspiring examples, however idealized in transit, of frontier freedom and individualism and democracy. But we should not forget that Europe has provided America with the norms and most of the forms of its political structure. Englishmen coming to America brought with them the traditions of Magna Carta and representative government, and without the precedents of the Puritan and "Glorious" Revolutions in the England of the seventeenth century, and the teachings of such Britishers as Milton, Locke, Burke, and Thomas Paine, the American Revolution would be incomprehensible. Our Declaration of Independence and our Federal Constitution were alike cast in English molds.

It was similar with Spaniards who settled in America. They were heirs of the political traditions of their mother-country across the Atlantic. As in Spain itself, so in Spanish America, a high degree of individualism and localism qualified and rendered largely illusory the authoritarian centralization which Habsburg and Bourbon monarchs sought to impose. Spanish rule was "despotic" only in name. Its actual exercise was decentralized, and there was a good deal of municipal, if not national, self-government. In fact, what strikes the historian as politically wrong with the Spanish colonial empire was less oppression from above than anarchy from below. There did eventually develop in Spanish America the same sort of self-consciousness and revolutionary movement which issued in the independence of most of English America. But it is indicative of the abiding strength of Spanish individualism, reënforced by geographical peculiarities, that, whereas the revolutionary thirteen English colonies have furnished the nucleus for a single great English-speaking nation in North America, revolutionary Spanish America has split up into as many as eighteen separate nations.

3.

The revolutionary period in America may be said to have extended from the revolt of the thirteen English colonies in the 1770's and 1780's, through the revolt of the Spanish colonies in the 1810's and 1820's, to the Canadian revolt of the 1830's. Yet that period of some seventy years could not have been so politically revolutionary for America if it had not been a period also of extraordinary strains and stresses throughout the Atlantic Community. As Professor Bemis has expressed it, "Europe's distresses were America's advantage." To which one might add, "Europe and America then, as before and since, were inextricably intertangled."

Hardly had the thirteen English colonies proclaimed their independence, when they dispatched agents to Europe to beg help in money and arms, especially from nations resentful of British predominance and anxious to counterbalance it. France, seeking revenge for her recent colonial losses to Britain, responded with alacrity to Benjamin Franklin's pleas. She allied herself with the American rebels in 1778 and supplied them with direct military and naval assistance, besides financial subsidies and loans. The response of Spain, which had not lost so heavily to Britain and which feared the spread of rebellion to her own colonies, was slower and more grudging. In 1779, nevertheless, Spain followed France in going to war with Britain, and though she sent no troops to fight alongside the forces of George Washington, she advanced nearly a million dollars to the United States and indirectly gave it military aid by engaging the British at Gibraltar, in Florida, and on the high seas. It was this large-scale war between France and Spain on the one side[1] and Great Britain on the other which finally induced the latter in 1783 to make peace and recognize the independence of the United States.

Regular diplomatic relations between the United States and Spain began in 1785, six years before Britain would receive an American minister. Though there were disputes about the boundary of Florida and

[1] Holland also participated, though in a minor way, in the war against Britain.

the navigation of the Mississippi, these were at least temporarily settled by the treaty of San Lorenzo, which Thomas Pinckney negotiated with Spain in 1795, the same year in which John Jay concluded his famous treaty with Great Britain.

As the Spanish government had feared, the revolutionary success of English-speaking Americans incited a spirit of emulation in Spanish America. Francisco de Miranda, the Venezuelan soldier of fortune who fought the British in Florida in 1781 and later toured the United States, became thoroughly imbued with revolutionary ideas and in 1810 led a South American revolt against Spain. Though Miranda himself was soon taken prisoner, the revolutionary movement, under other eminent leaders, such as Simón Bolívar and José de San Martín, overspread all Spanish America. Spain might have suppressed it, as Britain might previously have suppressed the revolt of her American colonies, if there had been no complicating factors in the Atlantic Community. The revolt of the Spanish colonies occurred, however, amidst the Napoleonic Wars in Europe, when Spain was struggling for her very life against the French; and by the time that struggle was over, Great Britain and the United States were favoring the independence of Spanish America and Spain was too exhausted to offer effective resistance.

ENGLISH AND HISPANIC AREAS OF THE ATLANTIC COMMUNITY

The United States obtained Florida from a hard-pressed Spain in 1819–1821. In May 1822 President Monroe signed an act of Congress appropriating $100,000 for expenses of diplomatic missions to "the independent nations of the American continent." Next month he formally received an envoy of Colombia, and in December 1822 an envoy of Mexico. In January 1823 United States envoys were appointed to Argentina and Chile, and in December of that year President Monroe enunciated to Congress the historic Doctrine which ever since has borne his name and been a guiding star in American foreign policy. "America for Americans," it might be entitled.

Yet the "Americans" were Europeanized Americans, and the Monroe Doctrine, while expressly pro-American, was not anti-European. Both James Monroe and his distinguished Secretary of State who drafted the Doctrine, John Quincy Adams, had full knowledge and lively appreciation of the Atlantic Community. They had no rancor toward Spain. They wanted "to cultivate friendly relations" with her and with all the other European nations.

4.

Meanwhile, the English-speaking peoples on both sides of the Atlantic had sympathized heartily and strongly with the popular uprising of 1808 in Spain (the "dos de Mayo") against the puppet regime which Napoleon and his armies had foisted upon that country. In the United States, for example, an enthusiastic assembly of Bostonians warmed themselves in January 1809 by drinking a round of toasts to the patriots of Spain, to the Spanish armies, to the Spanish people, to the imprisoned Spanish King Ferdinand VII, to Washington, to the Massachusetts legislature, —and the account of the celebration here ends with an "etc." Collections were taken up at Boston and elsewhere in America to help Spain in its "struggle for independence." As for Britain, it supplied the Spanish patriots not only with money but with troops, which under the command of Sir Arthur Wellesley, Duke of Wellington, and in coöperation with Spanish forces, carried on the struggle—the Peninsular War—until 1813 when the country was completely liberated. In gratitude, Wellington was made a Spanish grandee.

Spain continued after her "liberation" and the loss of the bulk of her American colonial empire to have a special interest and attraction for English-speaking peoples. Perhaps it was because she was no longer a great power, no longer feared or distrusted by them, no longer a serious rival or competitor of theirs in imperial expansion. Perhaps, too, it was because Spain seemed to them to be trying to introduce forms of government and a "liberalism" in harmony with their own; they naturally like to patronize any such country. Doubtless the romanticism of the nineteenth century had something to do with it. People who were brought up on the novels of Scott and Dickens and the poetry of Byron and Tennyson were in a mood to appreciate castles in Spain—and gypsies and the Alhambra. Spain appeared to have such a lot of sunshine and color, such a lot of the quaint and the curious.

At any rate, a century ago, waves of English tourists swept the Spanish coasts and the Canary and Balearic Islands, while English business men added to their interest in the Port wine of Portugal an even bigger interest in the Sherry wine of Spain. It was likewise then usual for Americans to include in their itinerary of Europe a sojourn in Spain. Some, like Washington Irving, George Ticknor, Henry Wadsworth Longfellow, and James Russell Lowell, brought back to the United States an admiration for Spanish culture, and in interpreting it they enriched American literature.

What we may call, despite recurrent frictions, an era of good feeling between the United States and Spain was climaxed in the early 1890's, as I have already suggested, by the celebration, on both sides of the Atlantic, of the fourth centenary of Spain's discovery of America. By this time, the independent

Spanish-speaking nations of the New World had reached maturity and were on particularly friendly terms with both Spain and the United States. While newly adhering to the Pan-Americanism urged by James G. Blaine and sponsored by the United States, they now prized more than ever their Spanish origins and background. It was symbolic that at that very time an especially cheap and privileged postal service, which is still in force, was established among the United States, Spain, and Hispanic America.

Here was a significant triangle, aligning America with Spain. And the long peace between the United States and Canada and the historic bonds between both and Great Britain gave promise of mutual understanding and coöperation among all the English-speaking and Spanish-speaking peoples within the Atlantic Community.

The promise has not been realized. Events of the late 1890's and in the present century have pushed it into the background and given new vogue to old misunderstandings and prejudices.

II.

Some Inveterate Anglo-American Notions About Spain

1.

n 1893, at the time of the Chicago World's Fair, a special cordiality marked relations between the United States and Spain. But it speedily passed away. In 1895 a rebellion broke out in Cuba, and American sympathy for the mother-country gave way to execration. Such sensational journals as those of Hearst and Pulitzer vied with each other in assailing Spain and demanding armed intervention of the United States in Cuba; and their inflammatory articles and editorials were echoed from pulpits and rostrums throughout the land. Came the sinking of the battleship Maine, no one knows how, in Havana harbor in February 1898: and two months later, despite earnest advice to the contrary from Stewart Woodford, the American Minister at Madrid, the United States was at war with Spain.

The Spanish-American War of 1898 cost Spain

the remainder of her overseas colonial empire, and the United States, much ill-will throughout South America. It embarked this country on an imperialistic career in the Pacific as well as in the Caribbean, and paved the way in Spain for the revolution and civil war of the 1930's. And, what is most pertinent to our present discussion, the propaganda by which the war was justified in the United States, served to revive and accentuate certain notions about Spaniards which had long been latent among English-speaking people. These notions, or "stereotypes" as Walter Lippmann might call them, have been so deeply implanted that the majority of Anglo-Americans find in them an adequate explanation of the Spanish Civil War and of the present regime in Spain.

Suppose you have recently lived three years in Spain, traveling about the country a good deal and talking with different sorts of people, and suppose you are known to be fairly familiar with the history of Spain. When you return to the United States you are asked questions, but you soon discover that the questions are mostly rhetorical. What is usually wanted is confirmation of preconceived ideas, not any new or upsetting information.

First, aren't Spaniards particularly cruel and intolerant? Didn't they treat Jews and Indians and Negroes very cruelly? In their barbarous bull fights, don't they show cruelty to animals? Haven't they been most intolerant with their notorious Inquisition and their persistent persecution of Protestants? Weren't their concentration camps in Cuba hideous and aren't Franco's jails packed with political prisoners?

Second, isn't Spain a despotism, dominated by Fascists with the support of an inordinately wealthy church, an insolent army-caste, and a grasping aristocracy of landlords? Doesn't it lack any middle class, and aren't decent Spaniards in exile or in prison?

Third, isn't the condition of the Spanish masses sorry beyond description? Aren't they poverty-stricken and illiterate, ground down by church, army, and nobility, and terrified by police? They do live in caves, don't they?, or in slums, and aren't they starving?

Fourth, aren't the Spaniards lazy? Aren't they too proud to work? Aren't they content with mere show, and isn't their favorite word *mañana?* Don't they have bad roads, bad inns, and broken-down railways?

Such are the questions and implied answers which I for one find current. One grows weary of trying to explain that Spain and Spaniards are not describable in simple, categorical terms. One is tempted to follow the example of a Foreign Service Officer I know, who has lived for several years in Spain. When that country comes up for discussion he merely shrugs his shoulders, smiles, and says, "Oh! Spain!!—bull fights, fiestas, castanets, gay colors, lovely señoritas, fruits and flowers." For, paradoxically enough, these also represent common notions about Spain, and mention of them will usually suffice to indicate that one knows all about it. Yet at the risk of generating more heat than light, I shall here attempt to contrast the simplicity of popular conceptions with the complex actualities of Spanish history and life.

At the outset, let me point out that our Western civilization, and the Atlantic Community as a whole, have always been characterized by national cultural differences. Spanish or Iberian culture does differ from French or German or Scandinavian culture, and each of these from Anglo-Saxon or Anglo-American; and the contrasts resulting from such differences have endowed the western world with much of its competitive and progressive spirit. At the same time, I must emphasize that throughout a thousand years of history the differences among the nations of western and central Europe, and of America, have been of less basic importance than what they have had in common. In contrast with Asia and Africa and a large part of eastern Europe, they have all developed similar historic traditions and shared in essentially the same civilization. It is only in modern times, with the emergence of rampant nationalism, that the common civilization has been obscured by a magnifying of national cultures.

2.

What is distinctive of Spanish culture, as over against other national cultures within our Western civilization, derives from peculiarities of habitat and history. Spaniards live in a land of high mountain ranges, desolate plateaus, swift rivers, and narrow coasts; they are used to much sunlight and comparatively slight rainfall and to extremes of heat and cold. Those who have come to America must feel themselves quite at home amid the Andes and pampas and along the hemmed-in Pacific coast. Physical environment has undoubtedly contributed to the individualism and independence which characterize Spaniards and to the marked variations from one Spanish province to another. Geography has prevented Spain from becoming a thoroughly unified country like England or France or even the United States, and it militates against any such regimentation of the Spanish people as Germans or Russians have experienced.

In fashioning a distinctive Spanish culture, history has played a role even more decisive than geography. Spain was an integral part of the old Roman Empire longer, and received a deeper impress from it, than any other country except Italy. Modern Castilian is closer to ancient Latin than French or even Italian, and Roman architectural remains are today more numerous and better preserved in Spain than in Italy. From Rome, moreover, Christianity was enrooted in Spain, probably by St. Paul himself, and certainly in apostolic times. Spanish culture is indeed an old culture.

It is also a richly variegated culture. For on its Roman and Christian foundations have been superimposed down through the centuries an abundance of additions by Visigoths, Basques, Catalans, Arabs and Moors. And while Frenchmen and other West Europeans crusaded for two centuries in faraway Palestine, Spaniards crusaded in their own country for over seven centuries. Not until the very year in which Columbus voyaged to America did Christian Spain finally capture the Moslem stronghold of Granada. And hardly was this achieved, and the country nominally united under Ferdinand and Isabella, when Spain became enmeshed not only in a huge American colonial empire but also in a dynastic European empire that included Germany, the Netherlands, and a large part of Italy.

What are outstanding features of the particular culture which has been fashioned by Spanish history and geography? In other words, what really distinguishes the Spaniard from other Europeans and Americans? With an intense national patriotism and a taste for adventuring abroad, he combines an extraordinary loyalty to a particular locality or region—to Old or New Castile, to Aragón or Catalonia, to Navarra or Vizcaya, Galicia or Asturias, Extremadura or Andalucía. Spanish life is not epitomized by a single capital city, as is French life by Paris, or English by London. Spain has not one, but many diverse cultural centers—Barcelona, Burgos, Granada, Pamplona, Salamanca, Sevilla, Toledo, Valencia, and Zaragoza, for example, as well as Madrid.

In his struggle against the physical handicaps of his native soil, and with his historical heritage, the Spaniard has developed curiously contrasting attitudes. He is an individualist to the extreme of anarchism; and however skeptical he may be in other respects, he takes very seriously the Christian idea of the dignity and equality of man. He has pride and is never obsequious. At the same time he is socially minded and has a deep sense of fraternity. He is very outgoing and courteous and hospitable, and he loves to talk and dance. Grave, he is also gay. Something of a fatalist, he yet is a crusader. With a stark realism, he mingles a mystical and frequently utopian idealism. He is still what Cervantes depicted over three hundred years ago, a composite of Don Quixote and Sancho Panza.

The average Spaniard is less "practical" about politics and economics than the Englishman or the Anglo-American. His "liberty, equality, and fraternity" are social, more than political concepts, and they do not necessarily mean democracy as we understand it. The Spaniard's respect for law is more elastic than ours, and his respect for form is firmer. He prizes art more than government or material wealth, and certainly one of the greatest and most distinctive features of Spanish culture is its art—its painting and sculpture, its literature and music. There is artistic form in Spanish dances and in Spanish bullfights.

Spaniards especially enjoy being heroic, while retaining a keen sense of humor. As expressed in a ditty they sang in their war against Napoleon almost a century and a half ago:

Viva la alegría!	Long live happiness!
Viva el bueno humor!	Long live good humor!
Viva el heroismo	Long live the heroism
del pueblo español!	of the Spanish people!

All nations are human. The Spanish is particularly so.

3.

Anyone who is familiar with Spanish life and culture, and reasonably objective in appraising them, is bound to regard the popular Anglo-American notions about them as largely legendary and to recognize that most of the notions, in so far as they have any validity, are as applicable to other peoples as to the Spanish. Take, for example, cruelty and intolerance. Both of these have been exemplified fully as much, if not more, in England and English America. Spanish treatment of other races, Indians and Negroes, compares favorably with English treatment. It was a Spaniard, Las Casas, who, not long after the first European settlement in America, earned the title of "Apostle of the Indies" by the eloquence and zeal with which he pleaded for humaneness toward the natives and opposed their enslavement and forced labor. Today, four centuries later, Indians are numerous and interrelated with Spaniards throughout South and Central America and Mexico, while in English-speaking North America they have been exterminated or sorely debased. As for Negroes, it was mainly English slavers who, for over two centuries, with indescribable cruelty, brought them to the New World; and their eventual emancipation has been achieved throughout Hispanic America without the civil war and lynchings which have attended and followed it in the United States.

It is doubtless true that Spanish jails are not "model jails," and that their inmates are likely to be treated less tenderly than prisoners in the United States. It should be borne in mind, however, that crimes of violence are proportionately more prevalent in Chicago or New York than in any Spanish city, and that no Spanish prison camp has ever been the scene of such atrocious wholesale cruelties as have latterly been practiced in Nazi Germany or Communist Russia. And incidentally, if one is inured to American football games, prize fights, and stock-car races, one should not be shocked by Spanish bullfights.

Spaniards have been intolerant. But what human beings have not? Jews were expelled from Spain at the end of the fifteenth century, which was two centuries after they had been expelled from France and England, and in the meantime they had been treated better in Spain than anywhere else. They are fully tolerated there now, and under the protection of the present Spanish government they have recently built a synagogue in Madrid and opened one in Barcelona.

True, Spain, throughout early modern times, was highly intolerant of religious dissent, and the semi-royal, semi-ecclesiastical court of the Inquisition has acquired in foreign countries a particularly bad reputation for its prosecution of alleged heretics and its condemnation of so many of them to death. Yet there was nothing unique about all this. Religious intolerance was a European phenomenon of the period, and it was practiced quite as sternly and harshly by Protestant England or Scotland as by Catholic Spain. Indeed, the victims of the Spanish Inquisition were fewer than those who suffered in Britain at the hands of Henry VIII, Elizabeth, Cromwell, and the Puritans, and from the drastic anti-Catholic penal laws which were not eased until late in the eighteenth century, and some remnants of which have survived to our time.

In the course of the last hundred and fifty years, the Spanish Inquisition has disappeared, as the English penal laws have lapsed, and Protestants have come to be tolerated in Spain, as Catholics in England. At the present time there are still certain restrictions on Protestants in Spain—for example, they may not mark the outside of their churches or give instruction in public schools—but such restrictions are fewer and less onerous than those which Sweden still imposes on Catholics. And while there is popular anti-Protestant prejudice in Spain, one has to acknowledge that prejudice against Catholics and Jews is not wholly lacking in the United States.

Our Anglo-American notions about the peculiarly

intolerant and cruel character of the Spaniard are simply distorted. It is likewise, in only lesser degree, with our notions about the peculiarly despotic nature of Spanish government and the peculiarly unhappy condition of Spanish society and economy. Deferring discussion of the complex political traditions and experiences of Spain until the next chapter, let us here briefly consider certain basic facts regarding its economic and social set-up.

Spain is now, as it has always been, a preponderantly peasant country, and a relatively poor country. Back in the sixteenth and seventeenth centuries, the influx of silver from America gave Spain the specious reputation of being wealthy. As a matter of fact, most of the silver flowed on out of Spain to purchase commodities from other countries, enriching them, and meanwhile so inflating prices in Spain that the consumption and therefore the production of its own goods diminished and the country's economy suffered accordingly. Matters were improved by reforming statesmen in the eighteenth century, during the reign of Charles III; and since the middle of the nineteenth century there has been a notable development of mechanized industry, especially in textile mills of Catalonia and ironworks around Bilbao.

Spain does have important mineral resources, but to no such extent as the United States, Germany, or

Russia. Nor does it have such broadly fertile soil as France. Most of its terrain resembles Arizona or New Mexico, rather than Iowa or Illinois; and from it the main part of its present population of twenty-eight million must eke out a living. This is done by hard work, for, despite conventional notions to the contrary, the average Spaniard is not indolent, and he is husky.

By hard work, supplemented by use of imported fertilizers, the mass of Spanish peasants have normally assured the country's self-sufficiency in food-stuffs—grain and meat, olive oil and wine, fruits and vegetables. Only in recent times have there been serious shortages, the cumulative results of Civil War, which put much land out of cultivation, and World War, which choked off the supply of fertilizers. In addition to the peasant majority, Spain does have a large minority of artisans and miners and workers in factory or foundry. It does have, also, a sizable and important middle class of professional and business men, shopkeepers and clerks. Altogether, in 1949, out of the total Spanish population of twenty-eight million, almost a third lived in cities of over 50,000 inhabitants, and two of these—Madrid and Barcelona—had over a million and a quarter each. This far from negligible urban population is as industrious in its way as the rural population, and it supplies Spain with important industrial and commercial supplements to agriculture.

Spanish economy could doubtless be improved, and social conditions bettered, by measures which have been proposed and in some cases inaugurated—for instance, extension of hydro-electric power, reform of land tenure, modernizing of agricultural methods, promotion of technical and technological schooling, etc. But supposing that all possible reforms of the sort are made, they still cannot completely overcome the physical handicaps of Spanish geography, nor can they be expected to raise the average standard of living in Spain to what it is in the United States.

4.

One hears much in this country of the vast wealth of the Catholic Church in Spain and of the riches which the Spanish nobility have wrung from the peasantry, and one is left to conclude that if only church and aristocracy were compelled to disgorge, the mass of Spaniards might be enabled to live quite comfortably. I know of nothing more mythical. Actually, there are very few personal or corporate fortunes in Spain comparable with the many in pre-war England or in contemporary America. Not only is the average Spanish peasant poorer than the average American farmer, but the average Spanish landlord or industrialist is poorer than his American counterpart, and the Spanish Catholic Church is much poorer than the Protestant Church of England or several other Churches, including the Catholic, in the United States.

However much land and income the Spanish Church possessed in early modern times, it has been reduced to the barest subsistence level by recurrent confiscations during the last hundred and fifty years—all with the avowed purpose of benefitting the masses. Today the church owns very little property, and the salaries of the clergy, from bishops down to curates, are less by a third or fourth than corresponding church salaries in England and the United States. The Anglican Archbishop of Canterbury receives $60,000 annually, while the Catholic Primate of Spain, the Archbishop of Toledo, has an income of $6,500. And you should see the dilapidated palace which is the residence of the Spanish Primate and sense its chill and poverty. A call on any other Spanish bishop or on the Papal Nuncio at Madrid would be similarly revealing; and as for the ordinary Spanish rectory, monastery, or convent, I cannot conceive of your finding anything of the sort in America so devoid of creature comforts and with such frugal food. If poverty is an apostolic Christian virtue, the Spanish clergy are outstandingly virtuous. And if they are a burden to the peasantry, it should be remembered that they are largely recruited from the peasantry.

But what about the richly jewelled vestments and reliquaries and chalices and the priceless masterpieces of painting and sculpture which you can see in Spanish cathedrals, say at Toledo or Burgos or Zaragoza, or in monasteries like Guadeloupe and Montserrat? The answer is that they do not constitute a usable wealth of the Church. They are national art treasures; and without the cathedrals and monasteries which house them, Spain would have to construct and maintain a series of municipal museums comparable with the Metropolitan in New York. As custodian of art treasures, the church may make dazzling display of them on special occasions, and a church sexton or guide may pick up a few pesetas by showing them to tourists, but they do not materially lessen the poverty of church or clergy.

Concerning the Spanish nobility, few if any generalizations can properly be made. As a class, it is, like the English nobility, proud of its titles, honors, and lineage, and traditionally loyal to monarchy and church. On the whole, while professing an ardent national patriotism, it is somewhat more cosmopolitan in outlook than the English nobility, somewhat less politically minded, and generally associated less with industry and more with agriculture, for Spain, in contrast with England, is primarily an agricultural country. The majority of the Spanish nobility do have landed estates, or "fincas." But they differ as to how they conduct their fincas and what they derive from them. A considerable number reside on the land and maintain the frontiersman's, or, if you like, the cowboy's, intimate relationship with primitive farm-life. Others are "absentee landlords," visiting their estates only occasionally, and entrusting to agents oversight of the tenants and collection of rents and dues from them.

There are wide differences in social standing between the elite of "grandees" and the numerous scions of lesser nobility, and also in the amount of landed property. A comparatively small number of nobles own big estates, particularly in Andalucía and Extremadura, where the nature of the land favors extensive rather than intensive farming. Elsewhere, noble estates are apt to be much more limited, or quite nonexistent; and a considerable number of Spaniards with noble titles possess no rural property at all but depend upon office-holding in state or army, or upon some urban business or profession. In any event, the Spanish nobility, with a few notable exceptions, is not what would be accounted "wealthy" in the United States. When you encounter a wealthy Spanish grandee or other aristocrat, you can be pretty sure that his wife or mother or grandmother has brought a dowry from Argentina, Mexico, Colombia, or elsewhere in Spanish America.

Of the lower classes in Spain, especially of the mass of peasants, there is a large measure of truth in the popular American notion. They are obviously poor, and many of them are illiterate.[1] Yet there are degrees of poverty, and distinctions must be made. Worst off are the peasants in western and southern Spain where the soil is poorest and large estates prevalent. In more naturally favored regions, such as Galicia, the Basque provinces, Navarra, Catalonia, and especially along the Mediterranean coast where citrus fruits are grown in abundance, peasant proprietorship of land is the rule and the peasants are materially better off. One finds in eastern and northern Spain fewer ragged persons, and fewer hovels and decayed villages, than one finds in the west and south.

It is true that around Granada you will find Gypsies living in caves—they have done so for centuries and

[1] According to the *Statesman's Year Book* for 1950, twenty per cent of Spaniards "over five years of age" cannot read or write. The percentage among the peasantry must be considerably higher, inasmuch as literacy is universal among the upper and middle classes and fairly common among urban workmen. "Over five years of age" seems, however, a curious qualification: if applied to the United States, it would obviously exaggerate illiteracy here.

apparently like it—and even around Madrid, where destruction of the Civil War has not been fully repaired, you may still find some cave dwellers. You will likewise encounter beggars here and there, and also young children with a minimum of clothes, or even stark naked. But you should not be too shocked by such findings in Spain, if you are at all familiar with the habitations and ways of living of a considerable part of the American population in Mississippi and South Carolina, or in urban slums and on marginal hill farms of New York State. The general average of personal well being, as of natural resources, is certainly higher in the United States than in Spain, but averages are apt to be deceptive and to leave out of account certain "imponderables" of personal well being.

One should be skeptical about stories of starvation in Spain. Spanish peasants see to it that they get at least a subsistence from the soil, and in a country as warm and sunny as theirs they do not require the clothing and shelter of a New Englander or Minnesotan. The disease of rickets is not one of Spain's ills; and the evident vigor, endurance, and general huskiness of Spain's conscript army, poorly clothed and equipped as it is, bespeaks an essentially healthy nation. And may I add a caveat about confusing intelligence with literacy? A Spanish peasant may be unable to read or write, but he is likely to be highly intelligent and to possess a real culture, and, along with it, a lively sense of the ridiculous.

Altogether, the popular Anglo-American notions, or stereotypes, about Spain and Spanish traits which I enumerated earlier, can best be described as faulty caricatures. In so far as they represent reality, they oversimplify or grossly exaggerate it, or else they render peculiarly Spanish what is broadly human. And in many respects they are as remote from reality as the conventional pictures of a miserly Uncle Sam or a well-fed John Bull. There is this difference, however, that whereas conceptions of John Bull and Uncle Sam change and are frequently attractive, our stereotypes about Spain are notably constant and chiefly repellent.

5.

How has this come about? Why, when Spain is mentioned in the United States, is the reaction so frequently and uniformly predictable? Why, particularly, do so many of our journalists and publicists and other supposedly well-read persons react with unquestioning, even passionate, repetition of those stereotypes? These are important questions, which have direct bearing on relations between English-speaking and Spanish-speaking peoples. I offer some suggestions by way of answer.

English-speaking people, whether in England or in the United States, have not only a common language but common historical traditions, and, among these, few have been more celebrated in English literature than the series of wars which England waged with Spain from the "glorious days of Good Queen Bess." It was in Elizabeth's time, back in the sixteenth century, that Englishmen from their island home, Shakespeare's "precious stone set in the silver sea," made the first successful inroads upon an imperial and seemingly all-powerful Spain. They helped to free the Dutch. They ravaged the Spanish Main and plundered Spanish treasure-ships. They vanquished the Great Armada and destroyed later lesser ones. They even ravaged Spanish ports. Altogether they broke the sea power of Spain and replaced it with their own. And presently, under Elizabeth's successor, the Stuart James, Englishmen, in defiance of Spanish claims, were settling in America.

Followed in the seventeenth century the bold buccaneering expeditions of Britishers like Admiral William Penn (father of the Quaker founder of Pennsylvania) and the egregious Henry Morgan, which alternated sacking of Cuba and Panama with seizure of Jamaica, Honduras, and Guiana. Then, early in the eighteenth century, as a result of the twelve-year-long war of the Spanish Succession, England secured Gibraltar, a monopoly of the slave trade, and special commercial privileges in Spanish America. When, twenty-odd years later, a certain Captain Robert Jenkins, returning to England from an illicit voyage to South America, related with dramatic detail how the bloody Spaniards had attacked his good ship, plundered it, and in the fray cut off one of his ears, and to prove his story produced a box containing what purported to be the very ear itself, popular indignation was so aroused that in 1739 Britain again went to war with Spain—this time for nine years. Repeatedly afterwards, open hostilities raged—from 1761 to 1763, from 1779 to 1783, from 1795 to 1802. During the last of these, Britain acquired the large Spanish island of Trinidad in the Caribbean.

It is doubtful whether this long series of wars from 1585 to 1802 provides, of itself, adequate explanation of the inveterate misconceptions about Spanish character which have persisted among English-speaking peoples. The series of wars which England waged with France was actually longer and more decisive; and yet for over a century now these two nations have understood each other fairly well and have usually coöperated. Even with the Dutch, the English waged a series of commercial and colonial wars; and certainly a deep sympathy has long existed between the two peoples.

What peculiarly distinguishes the Anglo-Spanish wars from Anglo-French or Anglo-Dutch, is the ardently religious and ideological character with which the Anglo-Spanish wars have been invested from the outset. They began at a time when western and central Europe was split asunder religiously by the rise of Protestantism and its consequent conflict with Catholicism. Fresh from successful crusading against Moslems, Spain, under Charles I and Philip II, stood forth as the champion of Catholicism wherever it was threatened—in the Netherlands, in Germany, in France, in England. On the other hand, England, under Elizabeth, became staunchly Protestant at home and extended aid to fellow Protestants abroad. Thus English nationalism was identified with Protestantism, as Spanish nationalism with Catholicism. Spaniards of the time felt that God had called upon them as a nation to defend traditional Christian civilization and the unity of Catholic Europe against Protestant forces of rebellion, greed, and destruction. Protestant Englishmen of the time were sure that as a nation they had a divine mission to uphold the pure Gospel and safeguard it against superstition, corruption, and papal despotism.

So the struggle between England and Spain, which

basically was commercial, colonial, and political, took on a religio-nationalistic complexion. Puritan propaganda, with which England teemed in the late sixteenth century and throughout most of the seventeenth, was vehemently anti-Catholic and anti-Spanish, and it implanted deeply in English national consciousness the conviction that Catholic Spain was the very personification of devilish cruelty and intolerance, deserving severest chatisement by those whom John Milton described as "God's chosen people, the English." It was pardonable, of course, for God's elect, in fighting the devil, to be intolerant and even cruel. John Hawkins, the pious pirate and slave-dealer, could justify his robbery of Spanish treasure ships by quoting Scripture to Queen Elizabeth: "Paul doth plant, Apollo doth water, but God givith the increase." But perhaps the most perfect summary of the Puritan attitude toward Catholic Spain can be inferred from the remark of Oliver Cromwell after his slaughter and enslavement of Irish Catholics: "I am persuaded that this is a righteous judgment of God upon those barbarous wretches."

In such circumstances, stereotypes of Spain and of Spaniards took form in England. From England they passed naturally to English America. The English settlers here were more solidly Puritan-minded than was the nation from which they came, and from the eighteenth century onwards they were involved in direct rivalry and conflict with Spain. After the United States obtained its political independence from Great Britain, the bulk of its people continued to fall back upon the stereotypes they had inherited from England to explain any difficulty they had with Spain and to justify their expansion at the expense of Spanish America. There was the trouble about trade on the Mississippi. There was the piecemeal and partly forceful acquisition of Florida. There was the Anglo-American role in "liberating" South America from the "Spanish yoke." There was the annexation of Texas. There was the Mexican War, with appropriation of California, Arizona, and New Mexico. There were the recurrent filibustering expeditions into Central America and Cuba. There was the Spanish-American War of 1898.

Before and during that War, evangelical Protestant pulpits in the United States vied with the "yellow" journals in indiscriminate denunciation of Spanish despotism, ignorance, backwardness, intolerance, and cruelty. And there is significance, as well as a touch of wry humor, in what President McKinley told a delegation of Methodist clergymen who were pressing him to acquire the Philippines: "I walked the floor of the White House night after night until midnight," he said, "and I am not ashamed to tell you, gentlemen, that I went down on my knees and prayed to Almighty God for light and guidance. . . . And one night late it came to me . . . that there was nothing left for us to do but to take them all, and to educate the Filipinos, and uplift and civilize and Christianize them, and by God's grace do the very best we could by them, as our fellowmen for whom Christ also died. And then I went to bed, and to sleep, and slept soundly. . . ." [1]

Many an Anglo-American still sleeps soundly after having his notions about Spain confirmed by resolutions of church conventions or by letters in the press from Protestant clergymen. But by no means do the notions, or stereotypes, owe their current popularity merely to clerical propagandists. Another effective agency has been the partisan writing of such eminent literary historians, during the last century, as Froude, Motley, Prescott, Markham, and Lea. Their sagas of the glorious exploits of liberty-loving Englishmen and Dutchmen against despotic Spain, and their philippics against the intolerance of the Spanish Inquisition and the cruelty of Spaniards in America, have been read with relish by two or three generations of our best educated people, and have been epitomized in articles and textbooks for popular consumption.

Nor should we overlook the influence of modern

---

[1] *Christian Advocate,* Jan. 22, 1903, quoted in C. S. Olcott, *Life of William McKinley* (1916), vol. II, pp. 108–111.

pragmatism. The general run of people in the United States may not know it by that name. They may not even have heard of William James or John Dewey. Yet their judgment about a thing is apt to be pragmatic: if it "works" or "succeeds," it is good; if it doesn't "work" or "succeed," it must be bad. Now obviously, in both material and political respects, the United States has proved eminently successful and therefore great and good. On the other hand, Spain has been defeated in one war after another; it has lost in turn its primacy in Europe and its empire in America; it has shrunken into a poor and politically troubled minor country. By the pragmatic test, it has clearly failed where the United States has succeeded, and consequently all the bad things that are said of Spain must be true.

Undoubtedly the political history of Spain during the last century has been singularly tempestuous and unfortunate, and has immensely reënforced Anglo-American notions about Spanish character. Englishmen have not understood why Spain has failed to establish and maintain an orderly continuous government of limited monarchy and democratic parliament like their own. English-speaking Americans have been distressed by the prevalence of army revolts and dictatorship in Spain and the apparent blasting of their hopes that it would become a peaceful, prosperous

Republic like theirs. Moreover, there has latterly been the partisan propaganda of Communists, with its wilful distortions and misrepresentations. This, especially when conducted under the cover of a "popular front" and the banner of democracy, has been accepted not only by "fellow travelers" but by many an innocent abroad as confirmatory of their worst opinion of Spain.

Spanish politics are indeed complicated, and in marked historical contrast with the politics of English America. I treat of them in the following chapter.

III.

Contrasting Political Traditions and Experiences

1.

A story goes about in Spain—I have heard a dozen different versions of it—to this effect: At the beginning of time, Spaniards prayed God He would give them sunny skies. "Granted," He replied. They next prayed He would make them brave and provide them with beautiful women. "Granted," He replied. Then they prayed He would give them excellent oil and wine. "Granted," He replied. Finally they asked Him for good government. "Ah," He answered, "I have already granted you three big favors. That is enough. If I gave your country good government, you would have heaven on earth." And, so the story concludes, from that day until now, Spain has never had good government.

The story has wit, but it fails to indicate that no other country on earth has been vouchsafed a political regime heavenly enough to be above criticism and beyond change. Even the Constitution of the United States, though lauded by some of our orators as "the most perfect embodiment of political wisdom," has undergone amendment on an average of every seven or eight years; and a large number of Americans, need I remind you, are chronically critical of the President and the Congress. It was acute criticism and dissent that brought on our American Civil War.

"Good government" is, after all, a relative term, and one subject to different and changing interpretations. What seems politically "good" to one age or country appears not so good or downright "bad" to another. Englishmen used to insist on their personal rights; now they accept a socialistic regime. The founding fathers of the American Republic talked much of liberty and little of democracy; now our slogan is democracy rather than liberty. Once upon a time, moreover,—back in the sixteenth century—our English-speaking ancestors acclaimed neither liberty nor democracy, but the political despotism of Tudor monarchs.

Similar alterations in the form and conduct of government, and in the degree to which it is regarded as "good," have marked the history of every country within the orbit of our Western civilization. They represent fluctuating fortunes in the historic Western conflict between the individual and the state, between the longing for liberty and the need of authority. Depending upon which of these is stronger in a particular time or place, the alterations vary. They may be more or less violent and revolutionary, more or less popular and satisfying, more or less enduring. In general, they are the political expression of national cultural developments and circumstances. And to the general rule, Spain is no more of an exception than England or the United States.

The Spanish masses are inclined to look upon government, except perhaps on strictly local government, as a nuisance, if not an evil, and to feel no such responsibility for its conduct as the average Englishman or North American has been taught to feel. This is not to say that they lack interest in politics. Indeed their interest in politics is intense. But it usually takes the form of uncompromising partisanship for one or another group of professional "politicos," and is more concerned with getting one's party into power than with guiding the exercise of power. Certainly within the last century and a half, political passion, even political violence, has been prevalent among Spaniards, and Spanish political leaders—the "politicos"—have included a disproportionate number of doctrinaire intellectuals fond of spinning fine political theories regardless of whether these can be woven into any practical fabric of government.

Explanation of the Spanish attitude toward politics, and of its divergence from the attitude of English-speaking peoples, lies not in any racial peculiarity but rather in special traditions and experiences of very long duration. Of abiding importance, for example, was Spain's incorporation for several centuries in the ancient Roman Empire, which allowed to towns and other localities some measure of self-government but whose central government, whether at Rome or Constantinople, was so far distant and so financially burdensome that it could command in Spain only a passive or grumbling loyalty.

Then, for a thousand years, during which national government took shape and acquired popular support in England, Spain had no central government at all, but was only a congeries of provincial kingdoms and principalities. During most of the thousand years, moreover, a large part of the country was under Moslem government, for which the conquered Christian natives had scant sympathy. What gave the mass of Spaniards a sense of coherence and eventually led to the ending of Moslem rule and the creation of a national state was less politics than religion. The Spanish church bulked larger in popular esteem than civil government, and the popular title of the first national sovereigns, Ferdinand and Isabella, was not "Spanish Kings" but "Catholic Kings."

Neither the Spanish church nor the newly established Spanish state was narrowly national, like state and church in sixteenth-century England. The church in Spain was international and Roman, while the state, instead of being centralized, was federal, embracing the partially autonomous kingdoms of Castile, Aragón, and Navarra, and counties of the Basques and of Valencia. In such a set-up, the ordinary Spaniard naturally continued to be more concerned with his locality and his religion than with national government.

This was further accentuated by Spain's becoming, under the foreign-born grandson of Ferdinand and Isabella, the center of an empire comprising extensive territories in both Europe and America. From the accession of Charles I in 1516 through the reigns of his Habsburg successors—Philip II, Philip III, Philip IV, Charles II—down to 1700, Spaniards were generally less concerned with national politics in their own country than with imperial policies abroad: colonizing and exploiting the New World; and struggling in Europe to preserve its religious unity and the integrity of the Habsburg family-possessions.

Alongside the imperial tradition bequeathed to Spain by ancient Rome and reënforced by Catholic

Church and Habsburg sovereigns, is the Spanish tradition of individualism approaching to anarchism. Its roots are in a fervent and mystical devotion to Christianity and its doctrine of the dignity of man. But it has been fostered by the tendency toward isolation which physical geography imposes on human living in Spain; and it has been nourished by the historical developments which have just been mentioned and which have distracted the attention of Spaniards from national concerns and centered it upon province, town, family, and self. The resulting individualism has rendered Spain a particularly unruly country, and local revolts and insurrections have been of fairly frequent occurrence. And from Spain the same tradition has been transported to Spanish America, accounting in large measure for the revolutionary disturbances which are so chronic there and which so bewilder, or amuse or irritate, the English American.

2.

Spain also has a tradition of representative, parliamentary government, quite as old as England's. Indeed, at the very time, in the thirteenth century, when English kings were being compelled to sign a Magna Carta and convene a "Model Parliament," charters of liberties and regular meetings of Cortes—

that is, representative chambers of churchmen, nobles, townsmen, and even peasants—were functioning as commonplace restrictions on royal power in the several Christian Spanish states: Castile, Aragón, Basqueland, Navarra, Catalonia, and Valencia. Though Spanish localism prevented these Cortes from being fused into a single national parliament, such as England had, they continued after the time of Ferdinand and Isabella to exercise a considerable control over taxation and legislation and thereby to limit monarchical authority. Charles I and Philip II could be no such despots in Spain as were Henry VIII and Elizabeth in England: the latter had to deal only with a single and usually sycophantic parliament; the former had to cope with several different Cortes, some of which, especially that of Aragón, were very stubborn and obstreperous. This made for a kind of anarchism in Spanish government, which not only seriously handicapped Philip II in his duel with Elizabeth, but helps to explain subsequent political events in Spain.

To counteract the disruptive individualism and localism, and to unite the country in support of imperial undertakings abroad, called for the assertion and enforcement of central national authority. This was not forthcoming from the Cortes, but it was from the crown. Beginning with Ferdinand and Isabella, the crown systematically utilized churchmen and army officers to back its authority. The Inquisition which the "Catholic Kings" established, though nominally an ecclesiastical court for cases of heresy, was actually a royal court for ensuring uniform obedience. And the conscript national army which the same sovereigns instituted was a prime agency for enforcing their will. To this, a second prime agency was added by Philip II in the form of a centralized administration of his disparate dominions under a faithful and disciplined civil service.

While Philip II and his Habsburg successors did not venture to get rid of the Cortes, as the Bourbon Kings of France got rid of the Estates General, Spain experienced in the seventeenth century no such revolutionary reaction against the crown as did England. As England was then exalting personal and parliamentary liberty against too much previous royal authority, so Spain submitted to royal authority as a remedy for too much liberty. And Spain, being a continental country in immediate contact with jealous neighbors, had greater need than sea-girt England for monarchical authority that could command a large standing army.

Consequently the older Spanish traditions of individualism, provincialism, and representative government were gradually overlaid—without being destroyed—by the growth of a new tradition of royal absolutism. The process was speeded by the forcible advent, in the early eighteenth century, of a second foreign dynasty, the Bourbon. This completed what the Habsburgs had begun. The first of the new line of Spanish kings was the grandson of Louis XIV of France, and, like that "Grand Monarch," he and his sons were intent upon centralizing government in their own persons and realizing the ideal of "l'état c'est moi." Philip V either abolished or ignored the Cortes; and his son, Charles III, earned the reputation of being an "enlightened despot" in a class with the contemporary Frederick of Prussia or Joseph of Austria. Charles III, through his equally "enlightened" ministers, Aranda and Floridablanca, and with the backing of a group of sympathetic noblemen, did impose on Spain a betterment of its economy and did infuse a new energy into the administration of its American colonial empire.

Something can be said, and much has been said, in behalf of the reforming spirit which swept over Europe and penetrated into Spain in the latter half of the eighteenth century, and which found spectacular culminating expression in the French Revolution of 1789. It is very doubtful, however, whether the "enlightened despotism" which was the carrier of that reforming spirit, and the precursor of revolution, was, especially in Spain, an unmixed good. Reforms were certainly needed, but not always those which a despotic monarch chose to decree. Charles III was too much actuated by abstract theories of contemporary foreign philosophers, and too little mindful of concrete conditions and traditions in Spain. By promoting a federal, instead of centralized, government, and by conserving the provincial cortes and topping them by a national parliament, he might have effected a compromise between authority and liberty which would have been consonant with the country's history and fruitful of popularly acceptable reforms.

As it was, the reforms of Charles III, including some that were unquestionably salutary, proved superficial and temporary. The product of "enlightened" despotism, they depended for continuing vigor on a succession of enlightened rulers. But the monarch who succeeded Charles III, his son Charles IV, could by no stretch of the imagination be deemed "enlightened." He was simply a stupid boor, dominated by a coarse wife and her paramour, the flashy self-seeking Godoy. To appreciate them, you have only to look at their portraits which Goya took such sardonic delight in painting. It was this queer trio, together with Ferdinand, the cringing intriguing heir to the throne, who turned over Spain to Napoleon Bonaparte and thus precipitated not only a war well-nigh ruinous for the country but also the internal political strife with which it has been afflicted ever since.

3.

This strife of the last century and a half is a different kind of thing—different in origin, nature, and result—from any that Spain had previously experienced. Its origin was not in native individualism and provincialism, but rather in the impact of novel foreign ideologies on Spanish tradition. Its result has been the creation of a new and militant division of Spaniards into two camps which may conveniently be labeled "Left" and "Right," or "revolutionary" and "conservative."

Let me here emphasize that the division was not indigenous to Spain. It was imported. When Spaniards began their revolt against Napoleon and the French in 1808, they were moved by a common patriotic impulse. As one of their own historians says, they were not then "absolutists or liberals, progressives or moderates. They were Spaniards; because of this they rose as one man; because of this they conquered."[1] Yet before they conquered they were already divided, and the ideological basis had been

[1] Juan Rico y Amat, *Historia política y parlementária de España* (Madrid 1861), I, 123.

provided by the so-called "Enlightenment" of the eighteenth century.

The Enlightenment's "transmission belt," so to speak, was Freemasonry. From England, lodges were instituted at Gibraltar in 1727, at Madrid in 1728, and elsewhere in Spain soon afterwards. To them flocked, despite repeated papal condemnations, a considerable number of Spanish intellectuals and nobles, as well as prominent state functionaries, and in 1767 a Spanish Grand Lodge was organized by Aranda, the chief minister of Charles III. However respectful the original English Freemasonry was toward church and political traditions at home, it was not so when transplanted to Spain. Spanish Freemasons absorbed from Hobbes, Locke, Hume, Voltaire, Rousseau, and D'Alembert a highly critical and skeptical attitude toward traditional beliefs and practices and a conviction that Spain must "catch up with the times," become "progressive," and get rid particularly of what the *philosophes* called religious "obscurantism" and "fanaticism." They were belligerently anti-clerical, and such outstanding Masons as Alba, Aranda, and Floridablanca were prime movers in the expulsion of the Jesuits from Spain and Spanish America in 1767.

The foreign influences brought to bear upon Spain in the eighteenth century by English Freemasonry, the

French Bourbons, and the imported philosophy of the Enlightenment, were quickened and magnified by developments in the early part of the nineteenth century. The armies of Napoleon brought with them into Spain the symbols and spirit of the French Revolution; and Joseph Bonaparte, whom they forcefully installed as King in place of the Bourbons, promulgated in 1808 a constitution and promised reforms patterned after those in revolutionary and Napoleonic France. Then, when the mass of Spaniards rose in patriotic revolt, British armies came to their assistance, bringing along English ideas of liberal, limited monarchy.

While Spaniards generally detested the French invaders and the intruded French King, and idolized Charles IV's son, Ferdinand VII, whom Napoleon had deposed and imprisoned, a goodly number of their leaders in the War of Liberation, already influenced by the philosophy of the Enlightenment and brought up in Masonic lodges, became convinced that Spain had much to learn from its English ally and even its French enemy and should revolutionize itself accordingly. It was Spaniards of this sort—"Liberal" Spaniards, as they are called—who, in a more or less self-constituted Cortes at Cádiz, adopted in 1812 a constitution providing for a form of government similar to England's and to what the French Revolutionaries planned in their constitution of 1791. The Cádiz constitution, however, was practically still-born. One of the first acts of Ferdinand VII, when the downfall of Napoleon permitted him to return to Spain two years later, was to annul the constitution and restore royal absolutism. He did so in the name of Spanish traditionalism as against foreign revolutionary liberalism. And as the mass of Spaniards were traditionally minded, and as the liberals among them, though very vocal, were relatively few, Ferdinand had his way, at least temporarily.

Five years later, the Liberal minority had another inning. Through the Masonic lodges and other secret societies—notably the Carbonari, imported from Italy—they infiltrated not only the civil service but the army and navy and brought on a revolt which in 1820 frightened Ferdinand into recognizing and swearing allegiance to the Cádiz constitution. But Ferdinand, always free with promises when he was scared, knew his people and the reactionary temper of post-Napoleonic Europe. To the latter he appealed for help, and it would have brought Russian intervention in Spain if the restored French monarchy of the Bourbons had not moved first. This time the French invaders were acclaimed by the Spanish populace. They easily overcame all resistance and enabled Ferdinand to revert to absolutism and wreak vengeance upon the Liberals.

Thus began, in the fifteen years from 1808 to 1823, a most fateful division within Spain between "liberals" and "traditionalists." In a sense, both these terms are misnomers. As I have tried to show, individualism, and the liberties of person, locality, and Cortes deriving from it, were old Spanish traditions, while the tradition of centralized absolute monarchy, which Ferdinand VII represented, was comparatively new. A Spanish traditionalist, in an older sense, might be a liberal. On the other hand, the new Spanish liberalism was not a natural indigenous outgrowth of the old Spanish liberalism, but a novel foreign importation, and the centralizing and anti-clerical policies which it stressed were quite in keeping with those of "enlightened" despotism.

4.

All this points up the most significant of all political contrasts between the Spanish-speaking and the English-speaking peoples, in particular between Spain and the United States. Our American ideas and practices of self-government—our liberalism and democracy—have been fashioned by a long and relatively peaceful evolutionary process. Our American Revolution was not so much an actual revolution as a reaffirmation and confirmation of results of the English revolutions of the seventeenth century, and these in turn harked back to the pre-Stuart and pre-Tudor medieval traditions of personal liberty and of local and parliamentary self-government. In other words, English America, like England itself, is a land where liberty has "gradually broadened out" and where time-honored popular experience and interest in politics have more or less inevitably produced a workable democracy.

Moreover, English-speaking peoples have been so permeated by this political tradition, by the very reason of its continuity and practical character, that they take it for granted and act upon it with only negligible dissent. Laborites and Conservatives in England, or Democrats and Republicans in the United States, may differ about specific legislation, but not about fundamentals of government. Laborites do not seek to replace limited monarchy with a republic, or Conservatives to replace parliament with a dictatorship. In the United States, there is no Royalist party, scarcely any Anarchists, or Fascists, and few Communists. Here we are all democrats, and "liberal" is a popular catchword. As a contemporary journalist says: "Out of some 140,000,000 people in the United States, at least 139,500,000 are liberals, to hear them tell it, 'liberal' having become a rough synonym for virtuous, decent, humane, and kind to animals.

Rare is the citizen who can bring himself to say, 'Sure, I'm a conservative. What of it?' And any American would sooner drop dead than proclaim himself a reactionary." [1]

In Spain, in sharp contrast, the word "liberal," to a large percentage of the population, is in very bad repute. It connotes a minority bent on revolutionary uprooting of native traditions and usages and forceful implanting of novel foreign ideas and institutions. And because of its historic association with Freemasonry, "liberal" is regarded in Spain as synonymous with "sectarian" and has taken on the opprobrious meaning of this term in the United States.

Nor has there been, during the last century and a half, any general agreement in Spain on fundamentals of government, such as obtains in England or the United States. While in these latter countries two major parties are accustomed to operate and compromise within a mutually accepted political framework, a deep and bitterly contested chasm has existed in Spain between "Left" and "Right," between "Liberals" and "Traditionalists." But this is not all. Spanish "Liberals" themselves have split into warring factions, one Royalist in the English fashion, another Republi-

[1] Robert Bendiner of the "liberal" New York *Nation,* quoted by Peter Viereck in the *Harvard Alumni Bulletin* of June 24, 1951.

can in the French style. Spanish Traditionalists have likewise disputed and fought among themselves. Some have been so devoted to the historic monarchy as to follow wherever the king might lead, whether to absolutism or to constitutionalism. Others, notably the Requetés or Carlists, especially numerous in Navarra and among the Basques, have wanted to temper the monarchical tradition with the traditions of church privilege, local autonomy, and federal government prevalent in the middle ages and the time of Ferdinand and Isabella. Still others, mindful of Spain's great military traditions, have looked to the army to provide a leader who, like Cromwell once upon a time in England, would suppress dissent and restore the country's prestige. And below and beyond the factions of Traditionalists and Liberals, it is important to recall, is the mass of peasants among whom anarchism, as well as patriotism, flourishes to an extraordinary degree.

With *national* politics a concern primarily of intellectuals and would-be intellectuals, and only spasmodically of the masses, it is natural that the contending Spanish parties and factions should be especially doctrinaire and unyielding. Set upon achieving the ideal, they have tended to ignore what is practical. Sure of the soundness of their program, they have been reluctant to subject it to debatable amendment.

Eager to make over the country as soon as possible in their own image, they have been impatient with seeking majority support through the slow and dubious process of popular education and peaceful persuasion, and have been tempted, rather, to resort to minority violence.

Such attitudes and behavior are modern, and not peculiar to Spain. They scarcely antedate the nineteenth century, and they are to be found in Italy, Portugal, Hispanic America, and wherever else an effort has been made to revolutionize traditional domestic institutions. In the case of Spain, the effort has encountered extraordinary difficulties. Originating under foreign influence, French and English, just when France and England were waging war on Spanish soil, and when the mass of Spaniards were fighting to free the country from foreign domination, the effort could hardly be popular. The "liberals" who championed it were a minority faction, and one which continued to be fostered by the tutelage and, on occasion, the active intervention of "liberal" England or France or both. It was one thing, moreover, to draft Spanish constitutions, providing on paper for liberal parliamentary government, and quite a different thing to put them into practice and make them function in the English or even the French fashion. The basic trouble was that liberalism of the imported variety, however good it might be in itself, or however traditional and acceptable to a country of export like England or the United States, was a divisive force when imported into Spain. Here, being in patent conflict with Spanish tradition and patriotism, it aroused militant opposition.

5.

In the circumstances, Spanish politics of the last century and a half could only be kaleidoscopic. Now you see a constitution and now you don't. Now you see a liberal government and presently you don't. Now you see an army general in control, and before long another—and another. And back and forth, in ever varying pattern, you see personal and partisan strife, interspersed on occasion by civil war and foreign intervention.

There was the Napoleonic constitution of 1808. It was a purely paper document, never put into effect. There was then the "liberal" Cádiz constitution of 1812. It was repudiated by Ferdinand VII on his return to Spain in 1814; and, reinstated by the revolutionary "liberals" of 1820, it was again repudiated by him in 1823, this time with the assistance of French bayonets and the support of the Spanish masses.

Ten years later, Ferdinand's death brought to the

throne his infant daughter, Isabella II, and thereby precipitated civil war. For his brother, Don Carlos, rebelled, claiming that under the Bourbon monarchy women were debarred from reigning and that therefore he was the "legitimate" king; and around him rallied armed forces of traditionalists in Navarra and the Basque region—the Carlists or Requetés. On the other side, as a counter-measure, the Regent for Isabella sought the support of liberals by issuing a "moderate" constitution in 1834, and, when this did not suffice, by promulgating a more "radical" constitution in 1837. Meanwhile civil war went on. Not until 1840 were the Carlists repressed, and then only temporarily and with the aid of foreign troops which the liberal governments of England and France sent into Spain. Henceforth for almost a century, a form of constitutional government was maintained in Spain, but with what changes and with what army dictation!

What, after all, held Spain together politically was the army; and its high command, rather than any parliamentary enactment, determined the country's political course. A virtual dictatorship, nominally "liberal," was established by a General in 1841, only to be replaced by the "conservative" dictatorship of another General, with a new constitution, in 1845. This was interrupted by a liberal revolt and the adoption of another liberal constitution in 1854, which was shortly superseded by the practical dictatorship of still another General with the delightful name of O'Donnell. Then, following his death in 1868, traditional Spanish monarchy was rocked to its foundations.

The nominally "liberal" Queen Isabella II, long without morals and now without army backing, fled to France. And while Carlists raised anew the banner of traditionalism in Navarra and the Basque provinces, yet another General, with the fascinating name of Prim, assumed dictatorial powers at Madrid. He set up a provisional government, sponsored a new liberal constitution, and then cast about for a monarch to operate it. After numerous nominees had sent their regrets, an Italian prince, Amadeo, son of the king who had despoiled the papacy, was eventually prevailed upon in 1870 to accept the dubious honor and come to Spain. But the day he arrived, Prim was assassinated; and thus deprived of his military backer, Amadeo could bring no order out of existing chaos nor overcome the popular prejudice against him as a foreigner. In 1873, thoroughly disillusioned, he abdicated and returned to Italy. Whereupon a group of radical liberals at Madrid proclaimed Spain a republic.

This first Spanish Republic lasted barely a year, during which brief time political confusion was worse confounded. The Republic had little popular support throughout the country; and where the Carlists or other Monarchists were not in control, anarchy reigned. Besides, the small Republican minority could not agree among themselves. One faction favored a centralized, another a federal, government; and within the year two different constitutions were accordingly devised.

In 1874, army generals once more took over, and by a *coup* restored the Bourbon monarchy, with Isabella's son, Alfonso XII, as king and with still another liberal constitution—the twelfth within seventy years. Weary of the previous political chaos, the classes as well as the masses generally acquiesced, and for the next twenty-five years a relative calm overspread Spain. At last, seemingly, a parliamentary system, modeled after England's, "worked," with "Conservative" and "Liberal" parties alternately winning elections and manning ministries. At one extreme, "reactionary" Carlists were subdued; at the other, "revolutionary" Republicans were held in check. The crown, too, regained popularity through the intelligent conduct of Alfonso XII and his wife, who was later Queen-Regent for their son, Alfonso XIII.

Yet the regime was not as substantial as it looked. Beneath the surface were still the criticisms and contentions of a variety of factions from Anarchists to

Carlists. And the leading statesmen—the "Liberal" Sagasta and the "Conservative" Cánovas del Castillo —not only felt obliged to manipulate elections but were dependent in last analysis upon the joint support of their respective military backers, Generals Serrano and Martínez de Campos.

From the period of the Spanish-American War in 1898 dates a renewal of domestic conflict. By this time the experienced leaders and defenders of the constitutional monarchy were disappearing. General Serrano had died in 1885, and General Martínez de Campos died in 1900. Cánovas del Castillo was assassinated in 1897, and Sagasta passed from the scene in 1903. Simultaneously, the losses which Spain suffered from the war in men, money, colonies, and prestige, were keenly felt and evoked widespread complaints and demands for reform. Simultaneously, also, the country was undergoing a good deal of large-scale industrialization, with accompanying unrest among urban workmen and spread of radical propaganda of republicans, socialists, and anarchists. The young King Alfonso XIII, with his English bride, narrowly escaped assassination in 1902, and there ensued an epidemic of strikes, riots, and disorder.

From 1914 to 1918, while most other countries were engaged in the First World War, Spain was enabled by its neutrality to better its economy and temporarily to allay political discontent. But as soon as that war was over and an economic depression set in, the sea of Spanish politics again seethed and became turbulent not only with the usual conflicting waves of liberalism and traditionalism, but also with fresh ones of socialism and even communism. To still them, Alfonso XIII had recourse to the same expedient which his father and grandmother had employed. He entrusted dictatorial power to an army commander. The resulting military dictatorship of General Primo de Rivera lasted for almost seven years, from 1923 to 1930.

The task proved too difficult for Primo de Rivera. He was perhaps not personally ambitious enough. He failed to build up any such supporting party as Lenin built up in Russia, Mussolini in Italy, or Hitler in Germany. He was faced by an ever growing opposition, and he was intrigued against by fellow army-officers and even by the King. Eventually he resigned and went into exile.

Only a year later, Alfonso was himself an exile. For the monarchy he headed and personified could not now withstand the loosed forces of revolution. On an April day in 1931, a self-appointed provisional government proclaimed Spain, for the second time, a republic. The new regime started off auspiciously and amid popular acclaim. As matters developed, however, its course proved brief and stormy and finally ended in tragic civil war. How this happened, I shall indicate in the next chapter.

But before proceeding with that, let me here insert a cautionary comment. From the foregoing summary survey of Spanish politics from 1808 to 1931, one may readily gather a grossly exaggerated idea of the significance of such an array of constitutions and so many swings back and forth between liberal government and military dictatorship. One should remember that while the ordinary Spaniard may be very excitable about politics, he feels less responsibility for actual government than does the Anglo-American. His prime concern is not government, but life. "Leave government," the Spaniard might say, "to the *politicos,* the police, and the army. So long as they don't unduly interfere with me and my way of life, they can do what they like with government and change its forms as they please. Give me an extra fiesta, and I'll cheer any of them." And as a matter of fact, Spanish life went its wonted traditional way pretty continuously and not too unhappily throughout the century and a quarter of noisy swingings of the political pendulum. Nor did the political fluctuations impede too seriously the country's material progress in industry and trade, roads and railways, as well as in agricultural production. Despite external political appearances, Spanish life continued to be a consistent and civilized life.

IV.

The Spanish Republic of 1931: Prelude to Civil War

1.

The Second Spanish Republic, ushered in with popular acclaim in April 1931, led a hectic existence for five years, and was then engulfed and swept away by civil war. About this Republic, and especially about the war which ended it, a curious mythology has developed and been widely accepted outside of Spain, particularly in England and the United States.

The story runs thus: The Republic represented an earnest effort of forward-looking, peace-loving, democratic Spaniards to reform their country and bring it abreast of other Western democracies, both socially and politically; to free the masses from poverty, illiteracy, and superstition, and to substitute for irresponsible monarchy or military dictatorship a government of the people, by the people, and for the people. This fine effort had the support of the vast majority of Spaniards, but from first to last it was opposed by the plottings and machinations of a reactionary oligarchy, consisting of army chiefs, landlords, and Catholic clergy. These were not strong enough, of themselves, to destroy the Republic, but they eventually did so with the help of Moorish troops and the military might of Hitler and Mussolini, accompanied by the utmost barbarity and cruelty. Hence, according to the story, the Spanish Civil War was a struggle between democracy and fascism, between "good" and "evil," from which "evil" temporarily triumphed in the dictatorship of General Franco. And the Spanish struggle was, of course, a prelude, a curtain-raiser, to the Second World War, in which the fascist powers assailed the democratic and peace-loving nations of the world and were finally vanquished. The moral of the story is obvious to anybody familiar with fairy tales: the "good," having triumphed over the "evil" elsewhere, must presently win out in Spain.

The story is essentially mythological. On a flimsy factual foundation, it has been built up and spread by propaganda, some Communist-inspired, some motivated by preconceived notions, and some merely reflective of partisanship, wishful thinking, or plain ignorance. In its current form, it obscures or belies what really happened in Spain during the momentous eight years from 1931 to 1939.

When the Republic was first proclaimed, it undoubtedly was popular. It was a more or less inevitable outcome of the collapse of Primo de Rivera's dictatorship and of the attendant discrediting of Alfonso XIII, and, as such, it was accepted not only by the masses but by the classes and by what was later termed the "oligarchy." The church certainly did not oppose the Republic. On the very next day after its proclamation, Angel Herrera, then director of the leading Catholic newspaper in Spain, *El Debate,* and now Bishop of Málaga, proposed the formation of a Catholic Republican party; and shortly afterwards the Primate, Cardinal Segura, Archbishop of Toledo, formally declared it "the duty of Catholics to accept the duly constituted government. The obligation of Catholics under the Republic," he naturally added, "is to send representatives to the Cortes who will defend the interests of the Church." What hostility there was among royalist landlords, was abated by a letter from the exiled King which was printed in early May 1931 in their favorite newspaper *ABC,* and which advised them to accept and coöperate with the Republic. Nor did the army raise any obstacle. Some of its chiefs, such as Generals Miaja and Queipo de Llano, and Ramón Franco, the brother of General Franco and its most famous aviator, were "leftist republican" by conviction, and others, such as Franco himself, gave loyal support to the Republic.

Yet anyone conversant with the checkered political history of Spain during the nineteenth century, and particularly with the stormy career of the First Spanish Republic, could have guessed with a high degree of certainty the fate of the Second Republic. After all, the *politicos* who operated it were hardly representative of the masses, to say nothing of the classes, that at first acquiesced in it, and they were divided among themselves into quarrelsome, doctrinaire factions of "liberals" and "radicals," "federalists" and "centralizers," "socialists" and "anarchists."

In the Second Republic, as in the First, the result was instability and disorder throughout the country and consequent alienation of important segments of its population. What proved worse under the Second Republic than under the First was the emergence of a faction of Communists and "fellow travelers," which took its cue from the revolutionary dictatorship at Moscow, and managed, through its superior organization and discipline, to infiltrate both Socialist and Anarchist factions and thereby to exercise a steadily growing influence. The Civil War, when eventually it came, was a truly domestic and popular struggle within Spain, but one whose stakes were of the highest international significance. Despite aid given to one side by Mussolini and Hitler, the Spanish Civil War was not a struggle between fascism and democracy, as these terms are understood in the United States. Such aid was given only after the Communist International —the Comintern—had obviously set out to transform the Spanish Republic into a satellite of Moscow. The central significance of the Spanish Civil War was its rescue of Spain from the fate which later befell the nations of eastern Europe and shut them up behind an Iron Curtain. The Spanish struggle was a prelude not so much to the Second World War as to the subsequent "cold war" and the struggle in Korea.

As was aptly stated, in 1937, by a brilliant Spanish physician who had originally been a strong supporter of the Republic, Dr. Gregorio Marañón, "If one were to ask a hundred persons today, regardless of whether they are Spaniards or not, why they were for or against one or the other of the two parties which are fighting against each other in Spain, some would speak of their democratic principles or their traditionalism, others of their militarism or anti-militarism, of their Catholicism or anti-religion, or of their neo-Catholicism, a curious species of the current ideological fauna, or perhaps even of their horror of the executions and air raids, or lastly of their personal approval or disapproval of the leaders of the respective parties. There are very few who base their reason on the true reason for the struggle, which is this: 'I defend the Republicans because I am pro-communist,' or 'I sympathize with the Nationalists because I am anti-communist.' Yet that is the crux of the question."[1]

2.

To make clear how this became the crux, and why there was civil war in Spain, reference must be made to actual developments under the Republican regime. At first, the leading figure in the Republic, the man who presided over its birth in April 1931, was Niceto Alcalá Zamora, a mild, middle-of-the-road Liberal. Benevolent and trustful by nature, he lacked the energy and forcefulness necessary to restrain extremist elements and to maintain public order during the transitional period. Less than a month after his assumption of the presidency of the "provisional government," and before any general election could be held, groups of anarchists and left-wing socialists were rioting throughout the country with impunity, and setting fire to churches and convents.

It was amid such disorders and revolutionary violence that a National Assembly, or Cortes, was elected in June 1931 to draw up a constitution for the Re-

---

[1] In *Revue de Paris,* Dec. 15, 1937.

public. The result was the return of a large majority of deputies of much more radical bent than Alcalá Zamora and his fellow moderates in the provisional government. There was only a little sprinkling of royalists and republican conservatives, and the only group which could be called moderate was that of Alejandro Lerroux, comprising at most some ninety deputies. On the other hand, there were 120 Socialists of various hues, including the "reddish" left-wing following of the Marxist trades-union agitator, Francisco Largo Caballero; fifty fanatically anti-clerical Radicals led by Manuel Azaña; and some fifty Catalan Nationalists, mainly of Radical tendency.

The Assembly met in August, and in December adopted a constitution framed and sponsored by the Radical and Socialist majority. This contained elaborate paper guarantees of personal liberty and provisions for democratic government through a Cortes, which would be elected by universal suffrage, and to which, as in France, the Cabinet directly, and the President indirectly, would be responsible. In these respects the constitution was merely a republican version and natural development of the monarchical constitution with which, since 1875, two generations of Spaniards had been familiar. In other respects, however, the new constitution was essentially revolutionary. Starting with the somewhat ominous declaration that "Spain is a democratic republic of workers," it struck at the religious Catholic traditions of Spanish life.

Not only was the church to be "separated" from the state and deprived of any public funds; it was to be subjected to the state, and secularism exalted above religion. While with one hand the Radical framers of the Constitution pledged religious freedom, with the other hand they abridged or erased it, especially in the case of the religious orders. Any order that required a vow of obedience to an authority other than the state was to be suppressed, and its property nationalized; any other order could be dissolved if the government deemed it a "peril to the safety of the state"; and no order might engage in education. Education was to be entirely secular, and marriage a civil affair. Divorce was legalized.

Whether one sympathizes or not with the provisions concerning religion which the majority of the National Assembly incorporated in the constitution of the Spanish Republic, they certainly did not represent majority sentiment throughout Spain. On the contrary, they aroused lively opposition and gravely weakened the Republic. As one of its foremost friends, the well known philosopher José Ortega y Gasset, said of the authors of the constitution, "These Republicans are not the Republic," and their work was "lamentable."[1]

The National Constituent Assembly, having completed in December 1931, however good or ill, the task of framing a republican constitution, for which it had been chosen, should then have arranged for regular parliamentary elections and adjourned. But its Radical and Socialist majority, aware of the rising popular opposition to them, postponed elections and prolonged the Assembly, and their sway in it, for two years longer. They thought they could thereby "educate" the country and make it accept their brand of "reform." To this end, they promoted the mild and moderate Alcalá Zamora to the honorary post of constitutional President of the Republic, and substituted for him as prime minister and actual head of the government the belligerently radical leader, Manuel Azaña.

Under Azaña and a succession of similar prime ministers—for even a common radicalism was not proof in Spain against personal politics—the National Assembly enacted much revolutionary legislation during 1932 and 1933. The large estates of the landed nobility were to be expropriated and broken up. The army was reduced and many of its officers

---

[1] In the paper *Luz,* June 16, 1932.

were retired. In response to demands of Radical Catalan nationalists, home rule was granted to Catalonia, with a local parliament and president of its own, while similar demands of Catholic Basque nationalists were ignored.

The central point of agreement between the Socialists and Azaña's Radical following was anticlericalism, and by concentrating upon it a clear working majority could be assured in the National Assembly. In 1932, the Jesuits, who conducted the best schools throughout the country, were banned and their property confiscated. In 1933 all remaining religious congregations were obliged to pay taxes and report regularly to the government and were forbidden to engage in industry, trade, or education. And the enforcement of these measures was attended by mob violence and police severity.

Against the course of events, opposition grew and expressed itself in many different ways. In August 1932 an army officer, General Sanjurjo, attempted a military and royalist revolt at Sevilla; there was as yet little support for such drastic action, and it was easily suppressed. In October, a definitely Catholic party, the Acción Popular, held an initial congress, with five hundred delegates in attendance; and in the following month, its leader, José Maria Gil Robles, while proclaiming its loyalty to the Republican form of government, indicated its willingness to coöperate with conservatives and royalists in a Rightist coalition for the defense of religion.[1] In the same month of November 1932, the most respected intellectual in all Spain, Miguel de Unamuno, rector of the University of Salamanca and a republican withal, protested publicly against the extra-legal police measures taken by the government; they were worse, he asserted, than the old Inquisition, which at least "was limited by a guarantee of rights."[2]

In May 1933 the Spanish bishops, who had hitherto showed notable restraint and patience, issued a collective statement condemning the government's interference with the rights and liberties of the Church; and in June this was reënforced by an encyclical letter from Pope Pius XI, the same Pope who not long afterwards would similarly denounce, for like reasons, both the Communist regime in Russia and the Nazi regime in Germany. Meanwhile the Radical Republican government at Madrid appeared unable or unwilling to maintain order in the country. In July 1933 the famous Barcelona newspaper, *Vanguardia*, editorialized on the situation: "It is useless to write or

---

[1] This coalition was known as the CEDA, convenient abbreviation of the cumbersome Spanish title, Confederación española de Derechas autónomas.

[2] In an address delivered at the Ateneo in Madrid, Nov. 28.

to protest . . . The citizens are expressing their growing indignation in every tone. But all in vain. Here in Barcelona there are murder, attacks, the explosion of bombs, shooting frays in the streets; and every day innumerable crimes are committed. What do the authorities do about it? At times they meet solemnly and mysteriously and then they merely make long statements to the press . . . In Catalonia anarchy is in control." From glancing at other papers of the time, one readily gathers that "anarchy" was not limited to Catalonia.

3.

Faced with an intolerable situation, President Alcalá Zamora at long last plucked up courage to dissolve the National Constituent Assembly and order the election of a regular Cortes in November 1933. This election was the first under universal suffrage, and of twelve and a half million electors, at least eighty per cent voted. The result was a popular landslide against the Radicals and Socialists. These together won only ninety-nine seats, while moderate Liberal Republicans of the type of Alejandro Lerroux secured 167 seats, and the Rightest coalition, the CEDA, secured 207. Lerroux was promptly installed as prime minister, and a halt was called on the nationalization of land and on the execution of the ecclesiastical legislation.

Yet the conservative reaction encountered a new set of difficulties from diametrically opposite directions. On one side, its supporters were by no means a unit. They included not only a group of moderate republicans, led by Lerroux, and a larger Catholic group led by Gil Robles and professedly republican. They also included two rival monarchist groups: one, the so-called "Traditionalist Communion" of Requetés, favoring a federal monarchy under the Carlist pretender to the throne; the other, the "Renovación Española," organized and led by such insistent advocates as José Calvo Sotelo and Ramiro de Maeztu, and seeking the restoration of the limited constitutional monarchy of Alfonso XIII. In addition, there was a new semi-fascist group, the Falange, headed by José Antonio Primo de Rivera, son of the former general and dictator, and recruited chiefly from youthful ultra-patriots impatient alike with monarchy and with republic. None of these groups commanded anything like a majority in the Cortes, and, though they had a common negative attitude toward the Radicals and Socialists, they could not agree upon any long-range positive policy, or ensure stability to any sort of republican government. During the space of fifty-seven months, from April 1931 through December

1935, the Republic had twenty-eight different ministries, an average of about two months' tenure for each.

On the other side, the popular conservative reaction, registered in the general election of November 1933, stimulated revolutionary activity and violence among the groups which lost the election. Through the Socialist and Anarchist trade-union organizations, abetted by Radical *politicos* and increasingly influenced by the small but compact group of Communists, an incessant denunciatory propaganda was carried on against moderate republicans as well as against conservatives and royalists. It produced an epidemic of strikes and riots, and in October 1934 an open armed insurrection against the Republican government on the part of socialist miners in Asturias and anarchist workers in Catalonia. Oviedo, the historic capital city of Asturias, was almost completely devastated, and in other towns there was much killing and looting. The regular army, whose chief of staff at the time, it is interesting to note, was General Francisco Franco, stood by the government; and at its behest, and after heavy fighting, he succeeded in subduing the rebellion and restoring a semblance of order.

The immediate upshot was popular acclaim of the Moderate prime minister, Lerroux, as Spain's "savior," and a rigorous penalizing of leaders of the rebellion. Before long, however, a quite different result emerged. The Leftist elements of socialists, radicals, anarchists, and communists put forth a flood of propaganda, justifying the rebellion and representing its forceful repression as a "martyrdom" of "progressives" by brutal "reactionaries." Moreover, the small Communist group utilized the occasion to infiltrate and gain influence in the other and larger Leftist groups, and to forward the "popular front" tactics which were then in vogue with the Comintern. For it is important to recall that in 1935 and 1936 Communists not only in Spain, but in France, the United States, and other countries, were proclaiming their devotion to democracy and their eagerness to coöperate in its defense against "reaction" and "fascism," and that many a right-wing socialist and many a sincere liberal took them at their word and welcomed them as political partners. And now that they were such good democrats and liberals, there couldn't be anything too bad about their economic and social doctrines. Communism at least represented a "noble experiment"; perhaps, in another American phrase of the time, it was "the wave of the future."

At any rate, by the end of 1935 all the Leftist parties in Spain were coalescing in a "Popular Front," and some of its most conspicuous Socialist leaders, such as Largo Caballero, Juan Negrín, Alvarez del

Vayo, and Fernando de los Rios, were expressing pro-Communist sentiments. As Largo Caballero put it early in 1936, "I am a Marxian Socialist, and Communism is the natural evolution of socialism, its last and definitive stage."

Meanwhile the conservative and moderate majority in the Cortes and in the country at large presented no such unity of purpose or program as did their opponents. Some, like President Alcalá Zamora, leaned over backwards in an effort to conciliate the Leftists. Others, like Lerroux, seemed to repent the energetic action taken against the Leftist rebellion of 1934; they yielded to criticism, wrung their hands, and did nothing of any account. Gil Robles and his Catholic party were distrusted by Liberals as being too far to the Right, and by Monarchists, especially the Requetés, as being too Republican and too far to the Left. And the Falange, with its noisy demonstrations, was a peculiarly disturbing element. In the circumstances, the instability of republican government could only continue; there were frequent changes in the ministry, and little was accomplished of a constructive character.

4.

Hoping to mend matters, the President, Alcalá Zamora, dissolved the Cortes and called for the election of a new one in February 1936. This time, the conservative and moderate forces were more divided and less resolute than they had been three years previously. On the other hand, the Leftist forces were now united under the attractive title of "Popular Front" and fully determined to win the election. They were pretty sure, in any event, to increase their representation in the Cortes, but to make doubly sure of an outright majority, the extremist elements among them resorted to terrorism during the election.

Even so, the outcome of the election was no landslide for the Popular Front. Indeed, according to the official count, its popular vote fell short of its opponents' by over half a million: 3,912,068 for the former; 4,633,905 for the latter. Yet, because the Leftist parties of the Popular Front had a common list of candidates, while the Rightist parties ran candidates against each other, the minority popular vote of the former obtained a majority of deputies in the Cortes, 258 to 215.

One of the first acts of the new Cortes was to force the moderate Alcalá Zamora out of the Presidency of the Republic and to put in the radical Azaña, with a radical ministry, and a program calling for rigorous enforcement of earlier measures against landlords and especially against the church, and for a gradual socializing of industry. This was the signal for "direct action" by anarchists, left-wing socialists, and communists. Alvarez del Vayo talked in Toledo of "Spain's being converted into a socialist Republic in association with the Soviet Union." Largo Caballero declared in Zaragoza that "the organized proletariat will carry everything before it and destroy everything until we reach our goal." Dolores Ibarruri, a Communist member of the Cortes, was so urgent in her pleas for revolutionary violence as to earn for herself the popular appellation of "La Pasionaria." Plenty of violence ensued.

Nor did the Radical government restrain its extremist allies. It was fearful of losing their political support; and in the name of liberty it allowed them license. The result was a rapid descent of the country into anarchy. Even such a staunch Socialist as Indalecio Prieto was appalled. "We Spaniards," he said at the beginning of May 1936, "have never seen so tragic a panorama or so great a collapse as in Spain at this moment. Abroad, Spain is a country classified as insolvent. This is not the road to socialism or communism but to desperate anarchism without even the advantage of liberty."[1]

Meanwhile the Radical government, in pursuit of an idealistic pacifism and in response to extremist

---

[1] Speech delivered at Cuenca, May 1, and published in *El Socialista*, May 2.

demands, was slashing the Spanish army and penalizing officers suspected of conservative sympathies. As many as 8,000 commissioned officers were retired on pittance pay, and leading generals were practically exiled to the Canaries or the African colonies. One of these generals was Franco, who had previously served the Republic as Chief of Staff and put down the Leftist rebellion of 1934. Now exiled to the Canaries, he warned the Popular Front prime minister in June 1936 of the mounting disaffection within the army. "I cannot fail to convey to you," he added, "the danger that this entails, not only from a strictly professional standpoint, but from that of all Spaniards in the face of the grave problems which threaten our country."[1] Franco's warning went unheeded, and, while destructive violence continued unabated in the country, disaffection and opposition spread in the army.

The civilian voice raised most bitingly against the Popular Front regime was that of José Calvo Sotelo, deputy in the Cortes and royalist leader. It was silenced on July 13, 1936. On that day, government agents took Calvo Sotelo from his home, and murdered him. This outrage precipitated army revolt and civil war.

---

[1] Melchor Fernández Almagro, *Historia de la república española, 1931–1936*, p. 167.

5.

The revolt occurred on July 18. Though it was hastened by the murder of Calvo Sotelo, it was doubtless planned before. That it was engineered and led by high army officers struck most English-speaking people as strange and shocking. In the United States and England, army chiefs have been so habitually subservient and so unquestionably loyal to civil government that the average citizen is not likely to understand or feel any sympathy for military revolts abroad; a revolt of the sort in Spain was apt to confirm his notion of Spanish "backwardness" and particularly to prejudice him against the Spanish army chiefs.

Here is a notable difference between English-speaking and Spanish- or Portuguese-speaking peoples. With the latter, whether in Europe or in America, it has long been the army, more than civil government, which has exercised predominance and been the guarantor of order and security against anarchy and subversion. The Spanish military revolt of 1936 was not a novel or extraordinary experience for Spain—or for Latin America. There were many precedents for it during the previous century, when army officers had repeatedly stepped in to overthrow a government which seemed unpopular or disorderly and to establish and maintain one that gave promise of being firmer and better. Such army revolts had not been exclusively conservative, much less "reactionary," in character and purpose; just as frequently, they had been liberal and "revolutionary." If they had produced a variety of dictatorships, they were also responsible for the overthrow of absolute monarchy and the introduction of constitutional government in Spain, and likewise for the creation of the republics of Latin America and Portugal.

The Spanish military revolt of July 18, 1936, was remarkably devoid of any particular ideology. The generals who led it were agreed only on the need of putting an end to the anarchical disorder with which the country was obviously afflicted and getting rid of the Popular Front government responsible for it. General Sanjurjo was a royalist and doubtless aspired to a restoration of the monarchy. General Queipo de Llano, on the other hand, was a liberal republican who blamed extremists for discrediting the Republic. General Mola had accepted and served the Republic, and so, too, had General Franco.

About Franco, some special comment is in order, for there is no figure in the revolt of 1936 and the ensuing civil war concerning whom there has been such widespread discussion. In background and career, he was very different from a Hitler, a Mussolini, or a Stalin. Unlike them, he came from a prominent family, received a good education, and was neither a fanatic nor a rabble-rouser. Unlike them, too, he was not a politician who paraded as a soldier, attended by a personal following of black shirts or red shirts. Rather, he was a professional soldier who got into politics by chance and then without commitment to any ideology. He certainly detested communism, but his opposition was motivated not by foreign fascism but by Spanish tradition and patriotism.

Franco was forty-four years of age at the time of the revolt. His father had been a naval officer and he himself had been trained and commissioned as an army officer at the famous Alcázar in Toledo, the Spanish equivalent of our West Point. For several years he served with distinction in Morocco, to whose native population he became deeply attached. His outstanding ability brought him rapid advancement in the army. As a major at the age of twenty-eight, he helped to organize the Spanish Foreign Legion; and six years later he was promoted to brigadier general in recognition of his part in the successful conclusion of the Moroccan war. From 1926 to 1931 he headed the military academy at Zaragoza, except for an interval during which he pursued higher studies in military science in France. Under the Republic, he was military commander successively in Galicia and in the Balearic Islands, and then Chief of Staff until removed by the Popular Front government and sent off to the Canaries.

It must be emphasized that the revolt of July 18, 1936, was directed at the outset not against the Republic itself but against a particular republican government. The leaders of the revolt issued their first proclamations in the name of the Republic. And in all probability, if matters had turned out as the leaders hoped, the revolt would have followed the pattern usual in the Iberian peninsula and Latin America: pronouncement by the army that a government must quit, imposition of a temporary military dictatorship, collapse and flight of the government, and eventual installation of a new civil government under previous constitutional forms and with military support, all accomplished in a short time and with little bloodshed.

Actually, however, matters turned out differently in the Spain of 1936. True, the revolt started off in the customary manner. There was the pronouncement, and there was prompt action by General Mola in Navarra and Old Castile, by General Queipo de Llano in Andalucía, by General Franco who on July 19 flew from the Canaries and took possession of Spanish Morocco, and only death in an airplane accident stopped General Sanjurjo. But there was no concurrent action in eastern Spain—at Barcelona and Valencia—

and by the time General Franco managed to get forces over from Morocco and effect their juncture with General Mola's, the Popular Front government was entrenched at Madrid and in no mood to surrender. Hence the revolt, instead of achieving a quick and bloodless success, led into a civil war which lasted almost three years and cost Spain immense loss of life and goods.

V.

The Spanish Civil War, and Foreign Partisanship

1.

In the Civil War which issued from the military revolt of July 1936, the insurgent generals had a large part of the regular Spanish army with them, and to them rallied numerous volunteers from among groups hostile toward, or disillusioned by, the Popular Front regime: Carlists (or Requetés), strong in Navarra and the Basque provinces, wedded to tradition, deeply religious and royalist; Falangists, dictatorially minded radical nationalists, with their principal backing in Castile and Extremadura; Moderate Liberals, especially among the upper middle classes, some royalist and some republican, including many who had belonged to Gil Robles's Catholic party. In the main, the insurgents, while representing a variety of opinions and aspirations, belonged to what in Spain was called the "Right" and "Center." As such they stood together in defense of church, private property, and public order, and against the anti-clericalism, socialism, and revolutionary trend of the "Left" and its "Popular Front." And as they were characterized by a militant national patriotism, rather than by any common political ideology, they appealed to the country at large as "Nationalists."

That the Popular Front government could resist the Nationalist insurrection for a fairly long time with considerable success, requires some explanation. Not all the country's armed forces went over to the insurgents. Most of the air corps, the greater part of the navy, and portions of the regular army, including several generals, stood by the government, in some cases because they were Leftist in sympathy, in others because they felt bound by their oaths of loyalty. Moreover, the government, before the revolt, had been arming, or permitting the self-arming, of sizable militia groups among its most ardent and vigorous supporters—socialists, trade-unionists, anarchists, and communists; and these groups, together with bands of ruffians, proceeded on the morrow of the army revolt, and over wide areas, to terrorize and wreak vengeance on clergymen, well-to-do persons, and everybody else suspected or capable of helping the revolt. It was a veritable reign of terror, and while it served to intensify opposition to the Leftists in regions held by the Nationalists, it also served to silence opposition in such regions as Catalonia and Valencia and to ensure their hold by the Popular Front.

Still another and somewhat paradoxical support the Popular Front government obtained. It enlisted the support of Basque nationalism. Until the military revolt of July 1936, the Radical Republicans had been as little disposed as their Conservative opponents to grant "home rule" to the Basques. They had granted a measure of autonomy, it is true, to the Catalans, but the leader of the Catalan Nationalists was a Radical extremist, while the Basque Nationalist leader, Aguirre, and the majority of his following were Catholic. Indeed, the Basque provinces were, and are, the most Catholic of all Spain. But once the Republican government was faced with actual military and conservative revolt, it finally acceded to Aguirre's demands and accorded the same measure of autonomy to the Basques as it had previously accorded to the Catalans. This explains the anomalous situation that whereas, during the ensuing Civil War, the mass of militant Catholics throughout Spain, including all but two of the Spanish bishops, arrayed themselves against the Republican regime, a large part of the Catholic Basques fought for the Republic. Their motive, of course, was nationalistic rather than religious.

Yet with its variegated support, from Catholic Basques to anti-Catholic Radicals and Anarchists, it is extremely doubtful if the Republican government could have resisted the insurgents beyond a few months, had it not received foreign assistance. This brings us to a subject that requires elucidation. For we have been told so often and so insistently about the aid which Franco received from Hitler and Mussolini that we are apt to forget or ignore two facts of prime importance: first, that the Spanish Civil War began as a strictly domestic conflict between Nationalists and "Popular Front"; second, that both sides to the conflict, the Republican government no less than Franco, sought and obtained foreign aid.

It is true that, almost from the start of the Civil War, the Portuguese government, fearful lest a victory of the Popular Front in Spain would lead to a triumph of communism throughout the entire peninsula, sided with the Nationalist forces and let them use Lisbon as a supply-base. It is also true that the Spanish Nationalists, lacking air power of their own, applied early to Germany for transport planes and bombers and that some ten or twelve of these were obtained and utilized to carry troops of General Franco from Morocco to Spain and to participate in attacks on Madrid at the end of August 1936. Yet it was not until three months later that Germany—and Italy—definitely sided with

Franco and gave much aid to him, and then only after the Popular Front Government was receiving extensive foreign aid, primarily from Communist sources or through Communist influence.

2.

The Russian Communist dictatorship and its international appendage, the Comintern, were greatly interested in Spain. Spain occupied a strategic position. It was the gateway to the Mediterranean, on one side, and, on the other, the link with Latin America. The triumph of communism in Spain would certainly be followed by its triumph in Portugal, and might prove decisive in Italy and France and across the Atlantic. Moreover, Spain, according to Marxian theory as amended by Lenin and other Bolshevik "theoreticians" (to use their own jargon), was more favorably conditioned than any other country of western Europe for the triumph of communism.

Marx himself had originally taught, we know, that a country could not be communized unless or until it was highly industrialized, with the largest part of its population constituting an urban proletariat. But that teaching was later combated by Lenin and turned on its head, so to speak, by the Russian Revolution of

1917. For it was not in industrialized England or Germany or Belgium or the United States where Marxian communism triumphed; it was in industrially backward and largely agricultural Russia. And if Russia was a natural field for communism, why not Spain? It, too, was industrially backward and largely agricultural.

The number of Spanish Communists, to be sure, was slight. But so was the number of Russian Bolsheviks at the time of their successful revolution, and the ensuing dictatorship could obviously be operated by a small minority if it was militant, disciplined, and ruthless. Besides, much the same popular unrest, partisan strife, and anarchistic disorder as had existed and been exploited by the Communist minority in Russia during the concluding period of the First World War, existed in Spain in the 1930's and were duly exploited by the minority of Spanish Communists. Through preachment and propaganda, infiltration into trade unions, and incitement to violence, they won converts and at the same time aggravated conditions; and through participation in the Popular Front they exerted in 1936 a growing influence on the Radical Government.

Then in July occurred the military revolt, threatening to overwhelm the Government and to dash the hopes of the Spanish Communists. Foreign comrades were naturally concerned, and they hurried to the rescue. On July 26, only eight days after the revolt began, an international Communist conference was held at Prague to concert plans for aiding the Popular Front forces in Spain. It decided to raise an international brigade of 5,000 men and a fund of a billion francs, to be administered by a committee of five: the Frenchman Thorez; the Italian Ercoli; José Diaz, general secretary of the Spanish Communist party; and two other Spaniards, Largo Caballero and "La Pasionaria." Six weeks later, on September 4, Largo Caballero became, by appointment of President Azaña, Spanish prime minister and minister of war, with virtually dictatorial powers, and with a full-fledged Communist as minister of "education" and the sympathetic Alvarez del Vayo and Juan Negrín as ministers respectively of foreign affairs and finance. In the same month Largo Caballero was visited at Madrid by Thorez, and a much more ambitious program for foreign aid was agreed upon than the one planned at Prague in July.

From France, where also a Popular Front government was being supported and influenced by Communists, the Spanish Popular Front was already obtaining important aid. In early August, through the special favor of the pro-Communist French Air Minister, Pierre Cot, a group of trained military pilots arrived from France; and in their wake came munitions and Leftist volunteers. It was but natural, therefore, that the execution of the program which Thorez arranged for in September with Largo Caballero should be centered in Paris. Here, in the Rue Lafayette, headquarters were promptly established for the extensive recruitment of foreign "brigades" and their equipment and despatch to Spain. In general charge was a committee, including, together with Thorez, the Frenchman André Marty, the Italians Palmiro Togliatti and Luigi Longo, and Klement Gottwald, the future Communist puppet-president of Czechoslovakia. In military command was a "General Walter," the pseudonym for a Polish Communist by the name of Swierczewski, who was actually a general in Russia's Red Army.

Meanwhile, from August onwards, aid came direct from Russia. Ship after ship brought thence to Spain's Mediterranean ports an ever augmenting quantity of munitions, rifles, machine guns, hand grenades, artillery, trucks. By February 1937 the average arrival was two ships a day from the Soviet Union. The supply was expedited by the establishment of full and close diplomatic relations between Largo Caballero's government and the Soviet dictatorship; and with the cargoes came Soviet agents, technicians, instructors, and propagandists.

From Moscow came also the Secretary-General of the Comintern, the Bulgarian Communist Georgi Dimitrov, to "advise" the Republican government in Spain and to take immediate charge of the arriving foreign brigades. The full history of these brigades has yet to be written. Certain facts about them may here be stated. Under instructions and coördinating supervision of the international Communist organization in Paris, responsibility for their initial recruitment, financing, and formation into national units was entrusted to the several Communist parties in Europe and America. In discharging this responsibility, care was taken to conceal or minimize the Communist character of the enterprise and to make it appear as one in behalf of a "popular front," to which stalwart devotees of liberal and progressive democracy should rally, the world over, to save Spain from "tyranny" and "reaction"; and to the prospective brigades were assigned such attractive (and disingenuous) names as "La Marseillaise" in France, "Garibaldi" in Italy, "Masaryk" in Czechoslovakia, and "Abraham Lincoln" in the United States.

The response was most gratifying. Enlistments were rapid and numerous; they comprised not only members of the Leagues of Communist Youth, but also many youthful and quite innocent idealists and the usual proportion of persons eager for adventure.

And, wittingly or unwittingly, many a liberal and philanthropic beneficiary of capitalism subscribed to funds which helped the Communist parties finance the enterprise.

Recruits for the brigades were usually brought to France, provided there with uniforms and equipment, and thence transported across the Pyrenees into Spain. Here they were drilled, armed, and organized as fighting units, chiefly at Albacete, where, from the end of October 1936, André Marty was in charge of their "indoctrination." What this was can readily be inferred from the account by a British recruit of his first impression on arrival: "the red flag was flying with the hammer and sickle of the Soviets, while the smallest children seemed to be able to sing the *Internationale* and give the clenched fist salute. . . . I began to think I had come to a Bolshevik state instead of a democratic one." [1]

By the end of 1936 there were several thousand members of the Brigades in Spain, and more thousands were added in 1937. Meanwhile, as early as November 1936, one of the brigades—the "eleventh" —was rushed to the defense of Madrid under the command of General "Kleber," whose real name was Lazar Fakete, and who, though Hungarian by birth,

---

[1] *In Spain with the International Brigade: a Personal Narrative* (London, 1938), p. 7.

had been a Soviet army officer for almost twenty years. The entry of the brigade into the Spanish capital has been described to me in a personal letter from a reliable eye-witness, a patriotic and democratically minded American citizen, who resided in Madrid during the whole course of the Republic and the Civil War. Let me quote him:

"I well remember," he writes, "the arrival in Madrid of the first of the International Brigades. It was a Sunday morning, the first of November I think. Most of the Republican artillery and the government had pulled out the night before for Valencia. About ten a.m. the column came up the Gran Via from the railway station. In their well-fitting khaki uniforms and bright new leather trappings they contrasted sharply with the bedraggled militia men in filthy blue denim overalls and tattered shirts. They carried long-barrelled rifles which we had not seen before and unusually long bayonets. From the muzzle of each man's gun fluttered a small red flag with the sickle and hammer. At the head of the column was a band playing the *Internationale.* The men, who marched at attention like well-drilled regulars, held their clenched fists in the air and sang the anthem of the Comintern. Their motorized equipment was also new and modern. It included rolling kitchens, light armored trucks, motorized machine-guns, trench mortars, small howitzers, ambulances, a mobile radio station, ammunition and other supply vehicles . . .

"At the intersection of our street they halted and fell out. Soon they began to pour into our office on the ground floor and open up the desks in search for stationery. Our hurried but discreet investigation revealed that all they were interested in was obtaining material with which to write home telling of their arrival in the Spanish capital. We did not get to see the addresses on the envelopes, but I surmise they were Slavic. . . . Suddenly the letter-writing was interrupted by a bugle call. The men hastily fell in and disappeared over the hill at double time in the direction of the front line close to the city. As they passed, another column, coming up diagonally from the railway station, fell in behind them. This was the second contingent. Half an hour later all Hell broke loose at the Front. . . .

"I have no reason to love Franco," adds the writer, "but neither have I reason to wish to see in the streets of Madrid, and other Spanish cities, a repetition of the ghastly scenes of slaughter and pillage that I saw enacted from July 18, 1936, on to the end of the Civil War, but particularly in the first two years of the conflict at the instigation and under the expert guidance of the trained assassins and saboteurs of international Communism. . . ."

There should remain no doubt of the early and extensive aid which the Spanish republican regime of Azaña and Largo Caballero received from Communist Russia and from both its allies and its dupes in France and other countries where Communist parties were active and "Popular Fronts" in repute. Nor should there be doubt about the central purpose of this aid. It was not to safeguard, except temporarily and nominally, a liberal, democratic Republic. Rather, it was to make Spain a Communist country, a satellite of Moscow. For this end, the Soviet Union and the Comintern not only patronized and "indoctrinated" the International Brigades. They had in Spain their own board of strategy, artillery school, anti-aircraft units, tanks, aviation, and supply service. Most significant of all, they had in Spain an elaborate secret police and a Cheka of their own. The Spanish commander of every military unit on the Republican side was attended by a "Commissar Politico," of equal rank, who represented Moscow. On Spain, Communist attention was certainly concentrated in 1936 and 1937; and from among the foreign Communists who went to Spain and actively engaged in the Civil War, a kind of roster can be compiled of those who since the Second World War have been dictators, or tried to be dictators, of Communist regimes. Thorez and Marty were there. Togliatti and Longo were there. Tito was there. And before they ensconced themselves behind the Iron Curtain, Dimitrov of Bulgaria and Gottwald of Czechoslovakia were there, together with high functionaries in the present Communist governments of Poland, Rumania, and Hungary.

3.

A special point must be stressed about the foreign aid which the Spanish Republican forces received from France, Russia, and international communism. Despite widespread belief to the contrary, it bulked much larger, during the first four months of the Civil War, than the foreign aid which the opposing forces received. When the revolt began on July 18, 1936, its military leaders did not anticipate a protracted civil war and felt little need of foreign assistance beyond the small number of airplanes they got from Germany. With these and with the regular Spanish troops whom they commanded, they at first made fairly rapid progress in overcoming resistance. On July 24 they met and formed a "Junta of National Defense." On September 29 they designated one of their number, General Franco, as Chief, or "Caudillo," of the Spanish State. By the end of October they were in effective control of the southern and western half of Spain and seemingly so near to the capture of Madrid that the Republican government, in fright, fled to Valencia.

But then Republican resistance stiffened. With the timely arrival of the International Brigades, Madrid was held and vigor put into the defense of eastern and northern Spain. A long civil war was now in prospect, and the Nationalists, as well as the Republicans, sought and obtained an increase of foreign aid. In this way, existing international tensions were brought into play in Spain, and gave to the Spanish Civil War the appearance of being a conflict between fascism and communism, or, in Anglo-American eyes, a conflict between fascism and democracy. Actually, in addition to being a struggle between Communists and anti-Communists, it was a struggle in the realm of European power politics.

The year 1936, we must recall, witnessed a peculiar cleavage and realignment among the European great powers, which, of itself and in its origin, had nothing to do with the trouble in Spain, but which eventually served to complicate it and obscure its real nature. Until 1935, Italy, under its fascist dictatorship, had usually coöperated with democratic France and Britain in upholding the peace settlement of 1919, while Russia's Communist dictatorship had held aloof from the Western powers and shown a willingness to coöperate with Germany even after it passed under

Hitler's Nazi dictatorship. In 1935, however, Communist Russia, becoming alarmed by Hitler's aggressive attitude, particularly the implied threat to itself in his recent pact with Poland, and also by Japanese aggression in Asia, shifted its foreign policy. It entered into a defensive alliance with France, and cultivated friendly relations with Great Britain and the United States. But in the same year, Fascist Italy was alienated from Britain and France by their opposition to the war it began in Ethiopia; and the moral and material support which the Western powers withheld from Italy was supplied by Germany.

In 1936, consequently, a new and rather precarious balance of power appeared. On one side were France, Britain, and Russia, constituting an informal and uncertain "Popular Front" coalition, and on the other side Germany and Italy, with Japan leaning toward the latter side, and the United States, in popular sympathy though not officially, toward the former. In March, Italy completed the conquest of Ethiopia, and Germany took military possession of the Rhineland. In October, a formal alliance was concluded—the so-called Rome-Berlin Axis—between Germany and Italy. In November, Germany and Japan signed an Anti-Comintern Pact, which was directed explicitly against international communism and implicitly against Communist Russia.

By this time, the Spanish Civil War was in full swing. Since August, allied France and Russia and the Communist International—the Comintern—had been giving military assistance to the Republican forces. Now, on November 18, Germany broke off diplomatic relations with the Republican government at Valencia and extended formal recognition to the Franco government at Burgos. Portugal had already done so, and Italy soon followed the German example; and before the end of 1936 all three of these countries, in the name of anti-communism, were openly providing the Nationalists with important military aid. A first contingent of Italian troops disembarked at Cádiz in December, and simultaneously Germany dispatched to Franco aircraft and technicians that he sorely needed and a body of well-equipped soldiers known as the Condor Legion. Subsequently, such assistance was steadily increased, until a year later, some forty or fifty thousand Italian troops were serving under Franco, and a fourth as many Germans, and from the Axis powers he was getting his planes and most of his munitions.

The reason for the intervention of Fascist Italy and Nazi Germany on the side of the Spanish Nationalists was not purely or even principally ideological. They undoubtedly were both anti-communist and anti-democratic; and their dictators, Mussolini and Hitler, might well imagine that the fascist type of totalitarianism they represented was indeed the "wave of the future" which, by overspreading Spain, would sooner or later engulf the whole Atlantic Community and wash back against the Soviet Union. Yet mere ideology had not previously stood in the way of coöperation between Nazi Germany and Communist Russia, nor would it later in 1939–1941.

No, the reason in 1936 was more immediate and mundane. It lay in the realm of power politics. The Axis allies could not afford to let the Spanish Civil War enhance the prestige and strength of Russia and France and cement their alliance. This was the very thing most likely to happen if the Republicans won the war. Germany and Italy had no predilection for Franco, and their primary purpose in helping him was to tip the European balance of power in their favor. Incidentally, of course, they hoped to get some tangible compensation for intervening. Italy wanted the Balearic Islands, and Germany was intent upon obtaining economic concessions in Spain and Spanish Morocco.

The fact remains that foreign partisanship, whatever its motives, did attend the Spanish Civil War. In Russia and the Western democracies, it favored the Republicans; in Italy, Germany, and Portugal, the Nationalists. Communism supplied the Republic with the International Brigades, and these stirred anti-Communists to furnish Franco with rival foreign detachments: a Joan of Arc unit from France, and small groups of Irish and "White" Russian volunteers.

Nevertheless, we must be on our guard against exaggerating the foreign assistance which the Spanish belligerents received, and against viewing it from the hindsight of the Second World War. The war in Spain was a forerunner hardly more than chronologically of the World War, and the alignment of world powers in the latter differed from that in the former. The Spanish Civil War was only incidentally an international conflict. It was first and foremost, let me again repeat, a *Spanish* war fought by Spaniards. The Spanish Republican armies were larger than the International Brigades, and the Spanish Nationalist armies were larger than the combined foreign forces that aided them. Nor was the foreign aid to either side constant or dependable. That Hitler, for example, was chary of aiding Franco is clearly evidenced in the report of a conference the Führer had on November 5, 1937, with his foreign minister and army chiefs, at which he stated:

". . . A hundred per cent victory for Franco was not desirable from the German point of view; rather were we interested in a continuance of the war and in the keeping up of the tension in the Mediterranean.

Franco in undisputed possession of the Spanish Peninsula precluded the possibility of any further intervention on the part of the Italians or of their continued occupation of the Balearic Islands . . . The permanent establishment of the Italians on the Balearics would be intolerable both to France and Britain, and might lead to a war of England and France against Italy—a war in which Spain, should she be entirely in the hands of the Whites, might make her appearance on the side of Italy's enemies. . . . General Göring thought that, in view of the Führer's statement, we should consider liquidating our military undertakings in Spain. The Führer agrees to this with the limitation that he thinks he should reserve a decision for a proper moment."[1] This was a year and a half before the Spanish Civil War ended, and though Germany did not immediately halt its aid to Franco, it thenceforth gradually reduced it. Hitler and his advisers obviously distrusted Franco, and we now have plenty of documentary evidence of German complaints against the Spanish Nationalists.[2]

On the other side, distrust of Communist Russia persisted in the Western democracies and militated

[1] *Documents on German Foreign Policy, 1918–1945,* Series D, Vol. I (Washington, 1949), pp. 37–39.

[2] *Documents on German Foreign Policy,* Series D, Vol. III, *Germany and the Spanish Civil War* (Washington, 1950).

against their coöperating with it in aid of the Spanish Republicans. This was true of Great Britain from the outset. British advocates of such coöperation were mostly confined to the Labor party, which had been crushingly defeated in the general elections of 1931 and 1935. The Conservatives were in power in Britain; and their Government, first of Stanley Baldwin and after May 1937 of Neville Chamberlain, was not only strongly anti-Communist but anxious to prevent international rivalries over Spain from bringing on another world war. It accordingly adhered to a policy of non-intervention in Spain and did its best to get the other great powers to do likewise. Response from Russia and from Italy and Germany was pretty hypocritical, but at least a show was made, from September 1937 onwards, of choking off foreign aid to the Spanish belligerents.

The situation in France was a bit different. Here the general election of May 1936 had installed a Popular Front Government, dependent on Communist support, sympathetic with the Popular Front in Spain, and tolerant of the flow of men and munitions across the Pyrenees to reënforce the Spanish Republican armies. The Government, however, was not a unit: the majority on which it rested included not only Communists but Radicals who were quite hostile to communism; and its head, Léon Blum, was a right-wing Socialist, pro-British in outlook rather than pro-Russian, and anxious to maintain a close entente with Great Britain. Besides, Blum was under heavy criticism from domestic opponents of "Popular Front" policies and activities. He therefore found it expedient to curtail or at least to camouflage French aid to the Popular Front in Spain; and after the Radicals forced him out of office in June 1937 and practically broke up the French "Popular Front," France joined Great Britain in the policy of non-intervention.

Already, in May 1937, the Popular Front regime in Spain, alive to the criticism in the Western democracies that it was a Communist front, attempted to allay the criticism by reshuffling its cabinet. The blatantly pro-Russian Largo Caballero was retired as prime minister and war minister, and succeeded in the former office by Juan Negrín and in the latter by the right-wing Socialist, Indalecio Prieto. The change, however, was more in appearance than in reality. There were still two Communists in the cabinet, and Negrín was a left-wing Socialist scarcely less pro-Russian than his predecessor.

4.

With any detailed account of the campaigns and battles of the Spanish Civil War, we are not here concerned. We need merely note its general course. After the initial Nationalist successes from July to October 1936, Republican resistance stiffened, as I have pointed out, and produced a kind of stalemate which lasted during the first half of 1937. Then the tide turned in favor of the forces of General Franco. This was the result of superior generalship on his part, of the counterbalancing of foreign aid to the Republicans by foreign aid to the Nationalists, and of growing popular reaction within Spain against the terrorism practiced by Communists and Anarchists, with consequent conflict and decline of morale within the Republican ranks.

Simultaneously the Nationalist forces were solidified, at least temporarily, by the creation of a unified political party. In April 1937 General Franco decreed the union of the monarchist and other groups supporting him in a single National party, the Falange. It should be remarked, however, that the Spanish Falange, as thus constituted, was no such compact, single-minded party as the Nazi in Germany, the Communist in Russia, or the Fascist in Italy. It was rather a confederation of diverse groups, including Requetés, Liberal Monarchists, Conservative Republicans, and Falangistas proper, all held together by the military and by common repugnance to the revolutionary "red" character of the Spanish Republic. Eventually they might fall apart, but for the time-being their affirmed union was advantageous to Franco and the Nationalist cause.

In the latter part of 1937, Franco accomplished the piecemeal conquest of Asturias and the Basque provinces in the mountainous north of Spain, and in March 1938 he turned east and drove a wedge between the Republican forces in Catalonia and those in the Valencia-Madrid zone. Then, early in 1939, he conquered Catalonia, including the key city of Barcelona; and remaining Republican resistance rapidly disintegrated. Azaña fled to France in February and shortly afterwards renounced the presidency; and with him fled the Catalan and Basque "presidents." The Republican General José Miaja, who had successfully defended Madrid since the beginning of the Civil War, now finding his position untenable, prepared to surrender the capital to Franco. In vain Negrín and the Communists urged resistance to the death. Miaja disarmed the Communists and obliged Negrín to flee into exile. On March 18, 1939, Franco paraded his victorious army in Madrid, and by the end of the month he was in undisputed control of all Spain and the tragic Spanish Civil War was over.

The war, lasting for almost three years, cost Spain a million persons killed, wounded, or exiled, and many millions in property losses. It ended the Second

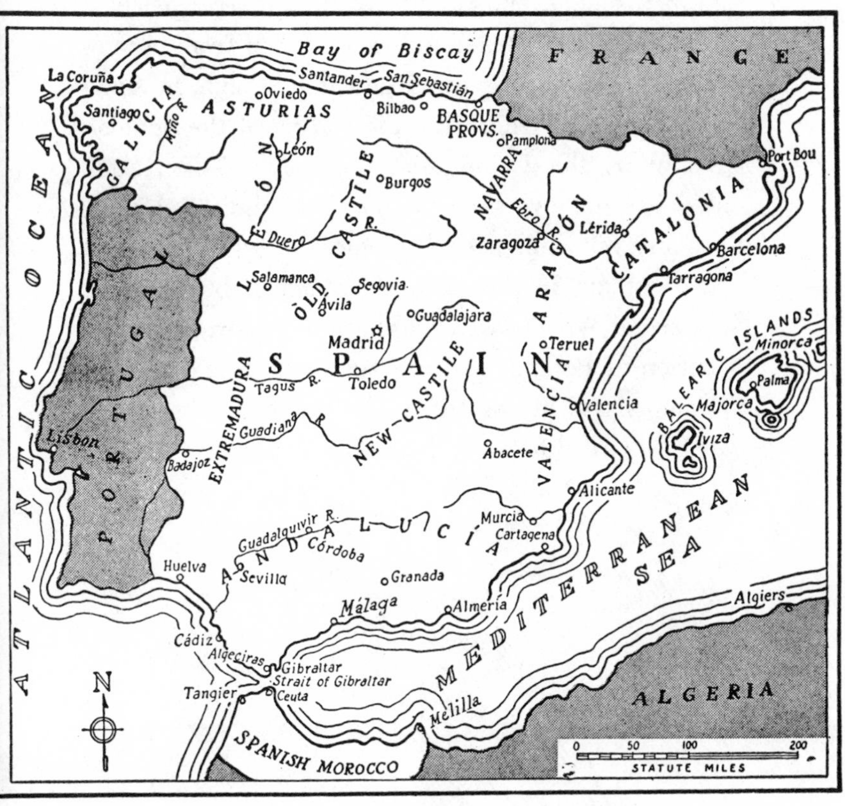
Bay of Biscay
FRANCE
ATLANTIC OCEAN
La Coruña
Santiago
GALICIA
ASTURIAS
Oviedo
Santander
San Sebastián
Bilbao
BASQUE PROVS.
Pamplona
León
LEÓN
Burgos
OLD CASTILE
NAVARRA
Ebro R.
ARAGÓN
Lérida
CATALONIA
Port Bou
Barcelona
Tarragona
Zaragoza
Duero R.
PORTUGAL
Salamanca
Segovia
Avila
Guadalajara
Madrid
SPAIN
Teruel
Tagus R.
Toledo
EXTREMADURA
NEW CASTILE
VALENCIA
Valencia
BALEARIC ISLANDS
Minorca
Palma
Majorca
Iviza
Lisbon
Guadiana R.
Badajoz
Abacete
Alicante
Murcia
Cartagena
Guadalquivir R.
ANDALUCIA
Córdoba
Huelva
Sevilla
Granada
Málaga
Almería
MEDITERRANEAN SEA
Algiers
Cádiz
Algeciras
Gibraltar
Strait of Gibraltar
Tangier
Ceuta
Melilla
ALGERIA
SPANISH MOROCCO
N
0 50 100 200
STATUTE MILES

Spanish Republic after eight years of inglorious and divisive existence, established a military dictatorship, and left a legacy within Spain of disillusionment, impoverishment, and bitterness. At a fearful price, it restored domestic order and saved Spain from becoming a satellite of Moscow. Ironically enough, in April 1939, the next month after the ending of the Spanish Civil War, the Communist dictatorship of Russia made its first overtures to the Nazi dictatorship of Germany for some such agreement as was concluded between them in the following August, bringing on the Second World War, making them partners in the partition of Poland, and eventually enabling Moscow to compensate its loss of a satellite in Spain by the gain of a half dozen satellites all over eastern Europe.

VI.

The Strange Story of United States Relations with Spain since 1939

1.

There is nothing stranger or more curious in the annals of United States foreign relations than the story of our relations with Spain during the last twelve or fifteen years. It can be explained in main part by reference to the "public opinion" which has attended and helped to shape its tortuous course.

In a democracy like ours, government depends in last analysis on public opinion. And public opinion on any particular question, including questions of foreign relations, reflects the information which people have, together with their preconceptions and desires. Prior to 1931 few of us knew or cared much about the internal affairs of Spain. Even in our colleges and universities, its history after the time of Philip II was usually ignored or only incidentally touched upon. In our newspapers, one might see now and then a stray item about King Alfonso's fondness for fast driving or about the physical ailments in his family. Whatever public opinion did exist in the United States concerning Spain was based not so much on any real or substantial information as on the heritage of stereotyped notions which I mentioned in an earlier chapter and which were given renewed currency during the Spanish-American War.

In 1931, rather suddenly, Spain began to figure prominently in our journals and radio-broadcasts, and the news that it was becoming a republic was popularly welcomed. For we Americans are predisposed to regard with special favor the adoption of a republican form of government by any foreign nation. It should produce abroad, we like to believe, the same workable type of liberal political democracy as we have at home; and in the case of Spain, it should prove especially beneficent. We are inclined to forget, however, that our American way of life and our political institutions have developed over a long period of time and can hardly be transplanted all at once into a country like Spain. A knowledge of Spanish history and conditions might have checked our optimism and made us dubious about the likelihood of the Spanish Republic's operating in the 1930's in the orderly liberal fashion in which our American Republic has long functioned.

As it was, our ignorance of life in Spain left us free to indulge to the full our bent for wishful thinking. We wished so well of the Republic and expected so much good of it that most of us overlooked or explained away the news which occasionally appeared in our press about disorder and instability and insurrection attending it from 1931 to 1936. Reports of the drastic anti-clerical legislation and of the burning of churches and killing of priests did elicit some reaction in the United States against the Spanish Republican leaders, but the reaction was largely confined to Catholic Americans, and this very circumstance contributed to majority dismissal of such reports as propaganda of apologists for a corrupt church and opponents of needful reform.

News of the army revolt of July 1936 came as a surprise and a shock to the general public in the United States, and when General Franco emerged as its Caudillo and was reported to be receiving military aid from Nazi Germany and Fascist Italy, pro-Republican sentiment here crystalized against him. We Americans have always had a repugnance to any military interference with civil government, and by 1936 we were well enough informed concerning Hitler and Mussolini to perceive in them arch-enemies of democracy and potent threats to world peace. The apparent combination of these fascists with a rebellious Spanish general indicated to most people in the United States that Franco and his Nationalists must be fascist and therefore "bad," while the Republicans must be democratic and therefore "good." And the Republic, being "good," must be backed, it was assumed, by the Spanish masses, while Franco, being "bad," could have within Spain only the support of a small selfish oligarchy of landlords and churchmen and could win only with foreign help.

That the Spanish Republicans were receiving extensive foreign help from the Russian dictatorship and international communism was less recognized at the time. But even if we had been fully informed about it, it would probably have had little effect upon prevalent public opinion in the United States. In 1936 and for the next two or three years, most democratic peoples, including Americans, were inclined to regard Communist Russia as being on the side of the angels in its professed opposition to fascism and benevolence toward "popular front" governments. If fascists were trying to destroy the Spanish Republic, why shouldn't democrats make common cause with communists in defending it?

We didn't go all out to defend the Spanish Republic. In the 1930's pacifism and isolationism were very popular in the United States, and by legislative enactment we were committed to neutrality in the event of foreign war. Hence as a nation we refrained from taking action against fascist aggression abroad and likewise from intervening in the Spanish Civil War. But lack of action signified no lack of words and wishes. Perhaps we sympathized the more completely with the Spanish Republicans and denounced Franco and his Nationalists the more hotly because we thereby got a vicarious satisfaction for not actually fighting.

At any rate, the bulk of public opinion in the United States during the Spanish Civil War, though opposed to active intervention, was distinctly partial to the Republicans and inimical to the Nationalists. In this position, to which it was naturally predisposed, it was confirmed by supposedly reliable information and also by partisan propaganda. Most of our journalists and publicists who followed events in Spain were certainly innocent of any intent to deceive or misrepresent, but they were apt to be innocent also of familiarity with the historical background essential to objective interpretation of what they saw or heard, and to reflect in their reporting the viewpoint expected by their readers or radio-listeners. In the course of the Civil War, our most important newspapers, such as the *New York Times* and *Herald-Tribune,* as well as our chief news agencies—AP, UP, and INS—had special correspondents with both Republican and Nationalist forces. But dispatches from the Republican side usually agreed better with what most Americans wanted to read and were therefore displayed more prominently, and bulked larger, than dispatches from the Nationalist side.

Moreover, the Spanish Republicans supplied plenty of propaganda calculated to appeal to "liberals" and "progressives" abroad and particularly marketable in the United States during the period of our "New Deal." Nor did such propaganda cease with the Nationalist triumph in Spain. On the contrary, it continued and exerted increasing influence after the end of the Civil War and into the next decade. For, following the collapse of the Republic in 1939, thousands of its Leftist supporters fled from Spain. Many of them took refuge in France, many in Spanish America, some in Russia. Leading figures scattered widely: Negrín and Largo Caballero in Paris, for example, "La Pasionaria" in Moscow, Prieto in Mexico City, Fernando de los Rios and Alvarez del Vayo in New York, and others in Montevideo, Havana, and London. Then, with the aid of Spain's gold reserve which they managed to bring out and deposit abroad, principally in Mexico, and which amounted to at least fifty million dollars, they maintained the form of a "Republican Government in Exile," and conducted an extensive campaign aimed at arousing such hostility to Franco's government as would induce foreign nations to overthrow it and put the Spanish Republicans back in power.

In the United States, the foremost propagandist for the exiles was Alvarez del Vayo. He made a happy connection with the New York *Nation,* and, in concert with its editor, Freda Kirchwey, utilized it as a major agency for publishing diatribes against "Franco Spain" and stimulating other "liberal" weeklies to do likewise. This type of propaganda was peculiarly influential with American intellectuals who liked to be thought of as "advanced"; and with less rarefied Americans it appeared to have the hallmark of authenticity. After all, a Spaniard should know what he was talking about, and Alvarez del Vayo was certainly a Spaniard, a charming and "progressive" Spaniard.

Thus, on top of the fragmentary and partial information which most Americans had of the Spanish Republic and Civil War, was superimposed during the Second World War and immediately afterwards the vehemently partisan propaganda of Spanish exiles. There was some counter-propaganda, but it was slight in comparison and quite ineffectual. The net result was that a large majority of our journalists and publicists took to echoing the charges that the Franco regime owed everything to Nazi Germany, that it was thoroughly fascist, that it was an active confederate of the Axis, and that it retained power only by most brutal methods. And to "Franco Spain" were attached the epithets which had long been popularly applied to the Spain of Philip II: "despotic," "intolerant," and "cruel," also "starving" and "doomed to fall."

Along with the partisan propaganda of Spanish Republican exiles, and reënforcing it, has been what I can only describe as the sinister propaganda of Moscow and international communism. This has been in the nature of deliberate, systematic, purposeful lying. During the Civil War it insisted that all the Leftist forces were peace-loving democratic liberals, when the Communist and Anarchist contingents were nothing of the sort. During the Second World War, after 1941, it insisted that the Spanish Government was pro-Axis, when it was really neutral; and it tirelessly repeated the most blatant lies about Spain's fueling of German U-boats, guiding of Axis warplanes, imprisoning of American airmen, and starving of its own people to supply Germany with food and munitions. In the United States this propaganda, if it had been confined to the *Daily Worker* and other outright Communist organs, would have had little effect outside the limited number of party members who religiously read those organs and thereby perhaps do penance.

But Communist propaganda reached farther. Its agents wormed their way into many a non-Communist publication and managed, with the help of "fellow travelers," to slant news, feature articles, editorials, and book-reviews toward the party line. If there is any doubt about this, let me refer you to the pages, during the war years and immediately after, of *PM*, for example, which was replete during the world-war years with all the lies which Communists could invent about Spain and with all the passionate partisanship which an Alvarez del Vayo was putting into the pages of the *Nation*.

And it must be recognized that a number of journalists on our more staid and conservative newspapers, and, I fear, some officials of our State Department, have taken their cue about Spain from the *Nation* or *PM*. What with the Communist propaganda and that of the Spanish exiles, which tended to coalesce, it is not to be wondered at that the reports from our innocents abroad and the commentaries of our innocents at home have proved not too innocent in effect. By the end of the Second World War it had become an extremely difficult, if not impossible, task to uproot the partisanship about Spain which had been implanted and nourished for ten years previously.

The propaganda had a cumulative effect, not only upon the popular American attitude toward Spain but upon the official relations between the two governments. As Al Smith would have said, "let us look at the record."

2.

At first, while the Spanish Civil War was still in progress and the propaganda to which I have just referred was only beginning, the prevalent attitude in the United States was one of neutrality. Americans generally sympathized with the Spanish Republic, without knowing too much about it, and the partisan Abraham Lincoln Brigade was recruited here. Yet we then had strict neutrality legislation, and our State Department on August 7, 1936, at the very start of the Spanish Civil War, publicly proclaimed that "in conformity with its well-established policy of non-interference with internal affairs in other countries . . . this Government will, of course, scrupulously refrain from any interference whatsoever in the unfortunate Spanish situation." That this conformed with American public opinion of the time was made abundantly clear as soon as the newly-elected Congress met, on January 5, 1937. The very next day it adopted a joint resolution, passed unanimously by the Senate and signed with alacrity by President Roosevelt, forbidding the export of arms, ammunition, and implements of war "for the use of either of the opposing forces in Spain."

By the time the Civil War was over, in March 1939, the anti-Franco propaganda was becoming intensified and exerting wide influence. But it was still not influential enough to cause democratic governments to ostracize Franco or to penalize Spain. On the contrary, Great Britain and France recognized the new regime and established full and friendly diplomatic relations with it in February 1939, and soon afterwards all the other democracies did likewise. The United States accorded full recognition to General Franco on April 1, 1939, and for six years afterwards maintained formal friendly relations with his Government and kept an ambassador at Madrid: first, Alexander Weddell, until our participation in the Second World War; then myself until the spring of 1945; and finally Norman Armour until November 1945. To Spain, under Franco, Ambassador Weddell on behalf of the United States Government and the American Red Cross, extended much material help in the way of foodstuffs, medical supplies, and shipments of fertilizer and petroleum in order to speed its recovery from the devastation and impoverishment of the Civil War and incidentally to fortify its resolve to stay out of the World War which so speedily followed the Civil War.

There is no doubt in my mind that General Franco

and his Government were determined from the beginning of the World War to stay out of it if at all possible. True, Franco in the recent Civil War had received important aid from the Axis powers, and it might reasonably be presumed that he would aid them in the World War. He did sign the Anti-Comintern Pact with them in March 1939. And when the German armies made quick work of France in the spring of 1940 and overran all western Europe up to the Pyrenees, Franco did assure Hitler of his friendship and loyalty, and of his willingness to engage in the war on the side of the Axis—*if* he got sufficient compensation: he suggested Gibraltar, a big portion of North Africa, and money and equipment for his army. What else could he have done to deter Hitler and the victorious Germans from immediately taking over Spain, as they had just taken over Denmark and Norway, the Low Countries and France? He surely knew he was asking a much bigger price than Hitler would pay, and yet by giving fair *words* to the Führer he warded off *action* by the Germans and also by Spain, and the more he was subsequently pressed for aid, the higher he raised the price.

No, the diplomatic exchanges between Franco and the Axis leaders which are now available to us in published form, show the Spanish Caudillo as an opportunist, perhaps, but not as a tool or ally of Hitler.

Franco knew, probably better than anyone else, how exhausted Spain was in 1939–1940, and how averse were the Spanish masses—and the Spanish classes also—from engaging in another war. Besides, until the spring of 1941, Communist Russia was practically an ally of Germany and its partner in aggression against Poland and throughout eastern Europe; and Franco and the Spanish Nationalists had less cause for loving Hitlerian Germany than for detesting Stalinist Russia. To become, even indirectly, an ally of Russia, would have seemed to them utterly fantastic, an ultimate *reductio ad absurdum.*

After the break occurred between Germany and Russia in June 1941, Communist propaganda obediently dropped the pro-German attacks upon the "capitalistic imperialism" of the Western democracies which it had been carrying on since the summer of 1939, and went all out against "fascism," once more coupling Franco with Hitler. On his side, Franco responded by assailing Russian Communism, calling for a "crusade" against it, and dispatching a division of Spanish "volunteers"—the so-called "Blue Division"—to fight alongside the German armies in their invasion of Russia. This alarmed both Great Britain and the United States, for it betokened Spain's departure from a policy of neutrality at least so far as Russia was concerned and quite possibly so far as the West was concerned. It was to help ensure Spain's continuing neutrality between the Axis and ourselves that, shortly after the United States entered the World War in December 1941, President Roosevelt sent me as his ambassador to Madrid. There I was for nearly three years, and the story of my mission was published shortly afterwards.[1]

I need not tell the story again. It still remains, after intervening criticism and documentary disclosures, a substantially accurate account, and it affords clear and concrete evidence that the Spanish Government of General Franco was not a catspaw for the Axis, but an upholder of Spain's own interests, which naturally inclined it toward coöperation with the Atlantic Community and particularly with the English-speaking nations. Spain's interest was to stay out of the war and be neutral, and it could feel surer of a neutral position if there was a counterbalancing of Axis forces by those of the Western Allies. Hence it interposed no obstacle to Britain's construction of a big air base extending out from Gibraltar into Spanish territorial waters, and it welcomed, rather than opposed, the Anglo-American landings in North Africa and our ensuing successes in Tunis, Sicily, and Italy. Moreover, Spain did not intern any of the 1,200 American

[1] *Wartime Mission in Spain* (New York, Macmillan, 1945).

airmen who force-landed in the country, but gave them refuge and permitted them to leave. It did the same with over 30,000 Frenchmen and sizable groups of Poles and Netherlanders, who passed through the country on their way to join the Allied armies. By special agreement in 1944 it provided us with important air bases, first for our commercial planes, and then for our military planes. Also, early in 1944, in compliance with our request, it recalled the Blue Division. And from within Spain, we were enabled, through our intelligence services—army, navy, and OSS—to organize and conduct in German-occupied France the espionage which contributed immeasurably to the success of our Normandy campaign.

Spain's neutrality during World War II was appreciated and publicly acknowledged at the time by leading Allied statesmen. Georges Bonnet, the French Foreign Minister in the first critical period, has written: "Toward the end of August 1939, M. Lequerica [Spanish Ambassador then in Paris, and now in Washington] indicated Spain's neutrality in the event of a European war. A few days later it was proclaimed officially. The Madrid government observed it completely during 1939–1940. Spanish factories made arms and planes for us. . . . French Morocco could be left entirely without defense and without the least danger, and the material and men sent to the Continent where they were so desperately needed. In June 1940 there was only one French regiment in Morocco and Algiers."[1]

In November 1942, at the time of the American landing in North Africa, President Roosevelt wrote personally to General Franco: ". . . Your nation and mine are friends in the best sense of the word . . . you and I are sincerely desirous of the continuation of that friendship for our mutual good . . . I believe the Spanish government and the Spanish people wish to maintain neutrality and to remain outside the war. Spain has nothing to fear from the United Nations. I am, my dear General, your sincere friend."[2]

In May 1944, the British Prime Minister, Winston Churchill, stated in the House of Commons: "There is no doubt that if Spain had yielded to German blandishments and pressure . . . our burden would have been much heavier. . . . In the dark days of the war the attitude of the Spanish Government in not giving our enemies passage through Spain was extremely helpful to us. It was especially so at the time of the North African liberation. . . . I must say that I shall always consider a service was rendered . . . by Spain, not only to the United Kingdom and to the

[1] Georges Bonnet, *Fin d'une Europe, de Munich à la guerre* (Paris, 1947), p. 82.

[2] C. J. H. Hayes, *Wartime Mission in Spain* (1945), p. 91.

British Empire and Commonwealth, but to the cause of the United Nations. I have therefore no sympathy with those who think it clever and even funny to insult and abuse the Government of Spain whenever occasion arises."[1]

In August 1944, following the death of Franco's Foreign Minister, Count Jordana, our own State Department issued a statement, expressing the "great regret of officials of this Government" and recounting major occasions on which, through his agency, Spain had been especially helpful to us.

Thus from 1939 through 1944, the Governments of both the United States and Great Britain publicly acknowledged the service that Spain, under General Franco's government, had been to them and to the United Nations during critical days. And from personal knowledge, I know that similar gratitude was expressed by the Provisional French Government which was set up at Algiers in 1943 and with which, from the outset, the Spanish Government exchanged diplomatic representatives.

3.

So far the record of official relations between the United States and Spain is consistent and of one piece.

---

[1] *House of Commons Debates,* May 25, 1944.

But in the spring of 1945 it suddenly and sharply changes.

Back of the change, and primarily responsible for it, was an intensification of the popular dislike of "Franco Spain" in the Western democracies and particularly in the United States. For several years previously, such dislike, natural enough in itself, had been spreading and deepening under the impact of partisan propaganda, but during the critical war years the allied Western governments had felt constrained to overlook it in the pursuit of what they deemed a necessary and desirable policy of friendship with Spain. By 1945, however, the situation was different. There was now less obvious reason for resisting the pressure of public opinion and propaganda. The crisis was passing. Spain no longer occupied a pivotal position between the Allies and the Axis.

With the end of the war clearly in prospect, prevalent public opinion crystalized in the belief that Franco was not only an anti-democratic dictator but a fascist of the same criminal stripe as Hitler and Mussolini, that we had catered to him long enough, and that our victory in the war against fascism would not be complete without getting rid of him along with his German and Italian partners. The very simplicity of this belief enhanced its popular appeal, and the Allied triumphs in 1945 imparted to it a special cogency and apparently rendered it translatable into action. In support of it, Spanish Republican exiles redoubled their propagandist efforts. Still more decisive alike with public opinion and Allied policy was the influence exerted at the time by Soviet Russia and international communism.

The dictatorship at Moscow, with its long memory, had not forgotten or forgiven the thwarting of its attempt in 1936–1937 to make a satellite state out of Spain. Now in 1945, relieved of danger from Germany and elated by the victorious advance of its armies into central Europe, it sought revenge against Franco. The time was ripe and auspicious. The United States and Great Britain, with which Russia had latterly been allied, were very anxious that the wartime alliance should endure as the cornerstone for a permanent United Nations organization to ensure world peace; and to achieve this major goal they were ready and willing to meet Russian wishes more than half way and to humor Stalin in many respects, for example with regard to "Franco Spain." And for such a policy of Russian appeasement there was now plenty of popular support in the English-speaking countries and also in France. It came from Communists and fellow-travelers, of course, but it also came from large numbers of people who in 1945 sincerely believed that Russia and the Western democracies were equally "peace-loving" and that mutual understanding and close coöperation among them were practical and easily attainable.

Moreover, changes in the directing personnel of the Western governments expedited the appeasing of Russia. In February 1945, when important concessions were made to Stalin at Yalta, President Roosevelt was a dying man, and he was attended at the conference by a new and inexperienced Secretary of State, Edward Stettinius, and by Alger Hiss, who had recently skyrocketed in the State Department. Then in April the American Presidency suddenly devolved on Mr. Truman, who had hitherto been concerned much more with domestic than with foreign affairs, and the Secretary of State whom he appointed in July, Mr. James Byrnes, was at the start scarcely better informed than his Chief. There was also a new, non-career Under-Secretary of State, Mr. Dean Acheson, who was a close personal friend of Alger Hiss and had the reputation at the time of being especially conciliatory toward Russia and hostile to "Franco Spain."

Significant government changes were not limited in 1945 to the United States. In July a general election in Great Britain supplanted the Conservative Government of Winston Churchill with a socialistic Labor Government headed by Clement Attlee, who on a visit to Spain during the Civil War was reported to have greeted the Republicans with the "Red" salute. Then in October 1945 a general election in France—the first in nine years—gave Communists over a quarter of the seats in the National Assembly and entrenched them in the French Government.

With these popular and political developments in mind, we may more readily follow the record of official United States relations with Spain from 1945. It is a record in striking contrast with the record before 1945, and quite contradictory to it.

I have no knowledge that Spain was discussed at the Yalta Conference in February 1945. But at the San Francisco Conference which convened in April to effect a permanent organization of the United Nations and adopt a constitutional Charter, the United States delegation expressed its "complete accord" with a resolution prompted by Spanish Republican exiles and presented by the Mexican delegation, which, though not mentioning the Spanish government by name, was clearly aimed at it. The resolution proposed to bar from membership in the world organization "nations whose regimes have been established with the aid of the armed forces of countries that have fought against the United Nations, as long as those regimes continue in power." The resolution, with concurrent affirmative votes of Communist Russia and the Western democracies, was adopted.

Then in July President Truman met Stalin and Attlee at Potsdam and joined them in a declaration, explicitly applying the San Francisco resolution to Spain. "The three governments," it said, "feel bound to make clear that they, for their part, would not favor any application for membership [in the United Nations] put forward by the present Spanish Government, which, having been founded with the support of the Axis powers, does not, in view of its origins, its nature, its record, and its close association with the aggressor states, possess the qualifications necessary to justify such membership."

In November 1945, our Ambassador at Madrid, Mr. Norman Armour, returned home, and no successor was appointed. In February 1946 the Assembly of the United Nations, meeting in London, affirmed and endorsed the Potsdam declaration.

In March 1946 the United States, in company with Great Britain and France, went much farther. In a "Three Power Statement," they called for the replacement of Franco's Government. "It is hoped," they said, "that leading patriots and liberally minded Spaniards may soon find means to bring about a peaceful withdrawal of Franco, the abolition of the Falange, the establishment of an interim or caretaker government under which the Spanish people may have an opportunity freely to determine the type of government they wish to have and to choose their leaders. Political amnesty, return of exiled Spaniards, freedom of assembly and political association and provision for free public elections are essential. . . ." The statement closed with a broad hint that if the advice of the three powers was followed, they might help Spain financially: otherwise, they might break off diplomatic relations with it.

This statement doubtless had a favorable popular response at the moment. It seemed so well-intentioned and sounded so pious. But the more one reflects on it, the more one wonders about it. It represents a complete reversal of the traditional American policy of not interfering in the internal affairs of a foreign country with which we are at peace, and a total disregard of the pledge in the United Nations' Charter not "to intervene in matters which are essentially within the domestic jurisdiction of any state." It likewise betrays a colossal ignorance of Spain, or else a blind subservience to Russia. For its authors should have known that Spain lacked any leader or organization competent to act on the advice so gratuitously given, and that, if an attempt were made to act on it, the result could only be chaos with communism as the chief beneficiary. Our statesmen seem to have been obsessed in 1945–1946 with the idea that Spain had to be "liberated" like Poland, Rumania, and Hungary—and later China—through the imposition of a coalition regime of democrats and communists. They quite overlooked the possibility that communists, once in, might behave like the proverbial camel, push out everybody else, and take full possession.

In the same month of March 1946, in which the naive three-power statement was issued, our State Department, apparently in an effort to justify it, published a selection of captured German Foreign Office documents purporting to prove the allegation that Franco's Government helped Nazi Germany during the war. The publication was tendentious and basically dishonest. For the State Department could have published from its own files more substantial proof that Franco's Government helped the United States during the war.

One example of the "screening" of the documents so as to inflame public opinion against Franco was the inclusion of the promise given by his Foreign Minister, Count Jordana, to the German Ambassador in February 1943 that, if the Allies should violate Spanish territory, Spain would join the Axis, and the omission of a similar promise given simultaneously by the same Minister to the American Ambassador that, if Germany should violate Spanish territory, Spain would join the United States and Great Britain. As it was, the "screening" must have been done a bit hastily, because it let slip through the mesh a document concerning a conversation of December 1943 in which the German Ambassador criticized Franco for being too pro-Ally and told him that this was "a very dangerous policy for Spain." Fortunately for the propagandists inside and outside our Government, few if any of our newspapers called attention to this particular revelation.

The publication had the desired effect—and more. Russia promptly cited it in support of a resolution which Dr. Oscar Lange, the delegate of the puppet Communist regime of Poland, presented at a meeting of the Security Council of the United Nations in April 1946. The resolution branded Spain as a "threat" to "world peace and security" and indicated the need of forceful intervention to remove the "threat." Mexico lined up with Russia and Poland in favor of the proposal, and so too, through Communist influence, did France. But it was a bit too much for the United States to accept. After all, one had to be extraordinarily naive or thoroughly committed to the "party line" to perceive in the Spain of 1946 a "threat" to world peace; and Dr. Lange's stories about Spanish stockpiling of atom bombs sounded pretty fishy. With United States' concurrence, therefore, the resolution, instead of being adopted, was referred to a subcommittee, which wrangled for several weeks over it and ended by substituting for the word "threat" the phrase "potential danger," whatever that meant. Whereupon Russia, as dubious as everybody else about the meaning, exercised one of its multiplying vetoes and killed the amended resolution in the Security Council.

The United States Government, still anxious to conciliate Russia and to allay its resentment over the failure of the original Lange resolution, sought a compromise by supporting new measures against Spain which the General Assembly of the United Nations adopted in December 1946. All members of the organization were now asked to express their very special disapproval of the Spanish Government by withdrawing from Madrid their ambassadors and ministers plenipotentiary and sending no replacements. Besides, the Spanish Government was formally debarred "from membership in international agencies established by or brought into relationship with the United Nations and from participation in conferences or other activities which may be arranged by the United Nations or by their agencies." Thereby Spain was excluded not only from international conferences of a political or economic nature, but also from those relating to aviation, health, agriculture, and the saving of life at sea.

To political and diplomatic ostracism, our government added an economic ostracism. It ostentatiously debarred Spain from the Marshall Plan, impeded commerce with it, and shut off both public and private loans to it.

Obviously, in the opinion of our government, the choice for Spaniards was to starve to death or to revolt against their government. For five years now we have expectantly awaited either one or the other of those dire events.

4.

The Spanish people have certainly been made to suffer economically. But they have also suffered in their pride and sense of justice. And as I prophesied six years ago in a memorandum I then presented to President Roosevelt and the State Department, most Spaniards, regardless of their opinion of General Franco, have resented the hostile foreign campaign against him, and, however much they have had to pull in their belts, they have not rebelled against him. There is no doubt that in 1950 he commanded a greater popular loyalty within Spain than he did in 1945.

That this is a fact and that it is attributable to the changed and erroneous attitude which the United States and other Western democracies took toward Spain in 1945 has gradually been borne in upon the popular consciousness. A growing number of Americans have come to perceive, especially since 1948, that it is not "Franco Spain" which threatens our peace and that of the world, but rather an aggressively expanding and thoroughly unscrupulous Communist Russia with its satellites and apostles abroad. Indeed, through an accumulation of hard and sorry experiences, our people have become quite disillusioned about international Communism and its directing dictatorship at Moscow; and as this is now our great and constant concern, we instinctively tend to regard any nation or group which takes a stand against it as a potential friend of ours. Thus, just as a large body of public opinion in the United States has come to look with favor upon the dictatorship of Marshal Tito in Yugoslavia, which, though professedly Communist, refuses to take orders from Moscow, so the military dictatorship of General Franco in Spain is nowadays viewed more realistically than in 1945. In existing circumstances we can better appreciate that Spain was the first country to wage successful war against Communism and to be saved from becoming a Russian satellite, and that it may prove very helpful to us, strategically and militarily, in any future world struggle into which we are plunged by Communist machination.

Recently, it should be noted, the shift of opinion about Spain has been accompanied by a decline of the quantity and influence of the partisan propaganda which was so effective during and immediately after the World War. The Spanish Republican exiles have latterly taken to quarreling bitterly among themselves —Negrín and Alvarez del Vayo against Prieto, for example—and they are now largely ignored. Nowadays, too, Communist propaganda is more easily detected and discredited than it used to be.

Interestingly enough, the reaction of the last two or three years in favor of Spain has been strongest in our armed services and in Congress, and has only hesitantly and reluctantly been acted upon at the White House and in the State Department. In March 1948 the House of Representatives voted, 149 to 52, to include Spain in the Marshall Plan, but the State Department prevailed upon the Senate to withhold its assent. In October 1948 General Marshall, who, though Secretary of State at the time, was primarily an army officer, admitted in a press interview that "the United Nations' ban on accrediting ambassadors to Franco Spain is no longer justified," but in January 1949 Marshall was succeeded as head of the State

Department by Dean Acheson. Mr. Acheson was still quite adamant about Spain. In March 1949 he insisted on its exclusion from the North Atlantic Defense Pact, to which all other North Atlantic countries were admitted, including Portugal and Iceland, and also Italy and Luxemburg. In May, a few days before the United Nations Assembly was to consider a Latin-American resolution for lifting the 1946 ban on Spain, he expressed anew and forcefully his hostility to General Franco's government. Then, when the resolution came to a vote in the Assembly, the United States delegation did not go along with the Latin Americans but, in company with fifteen other delegations, abstained from voting and thereby ensured its defeat.

During the next months, however, the Secretary of State, under congressional and army pressure, gradually softened. By January 1950 he felt constrained to confess publicly that a mistake had been made about Spain. In an open letter to Senator Connally, after strangely remarking that "the United States has long questioned the wisdom and efficacy of the action recommended in the 1946 resolution," he went on to say: "It is now clear that this action has not only failed in its intended purpose but has served to strengthen the position of the present regime. . . . In our view, the withdrawal of ambassadors from Spain as a means of political pressure was a mistaken departure from established principle. . . . The United States is therefore prepared to vote for a resolution in the General Assembly which will leave members free to send an ambassador or minister to Spain if they choose. We would do this . . ." In the same letter the chastened Secretary indicated still another veering—a kind of tack backwards—of the policy of the United States toward Spain. We would now, after denouncing General Franco's government and urging its overthrow, seek a rapprochement with it. In Mr. Acheson's words: "first, there is no sign of an alternative. . . ; second, the internal position of the present regime is strong and enjoys the support of many who, although they might prefer another form of government or chief of state, fear that chaos and civil strife would follow a move to overthrow the government; third, Spain is a part of Western Europe which should not be permanently isolated from normal relations with that area. . . ."

So, in January 1950, realism was reëmerging in our State Department. It was by no means fully ascendant, however. Secretary Acheson attached to his famous letter of that month a qualifying proviso that restoration of normal diplomatic relations "would in no sense signify approval of the regime in Spain"; and he stuck to the previous policy of economic ostracism. In April he vigorously opposed a pending measure in the Senate which would have made Spain eligible for Marshall Plan aid and authorized a loan of fifty million dollars to it from the Export-Import Bank. If adopted, the Secretary wrote to Senator Connally, it "would undermine the concept of democracy in Western Europe." It was defeated by only seven votes, however, and then with the understanding that Spain could negotiate loans direct with the Export-Import Bank. But when request was made of the Bank for a few small loans, chiefly for the purchase of fertilizer, they were refused.

The Senate returned to the charge. On August 1, 1950, by a vote of 65 to 15 it adopted a resolution providing for a loan of a hundred million dollars to Spain. The Secretary of State managed to have it sidetracked temporarily in the House of Representatives. Then when both Houses of Congress, by overwhelming majorities, voted in September a loan of sixty-two and a half millions, President Truman hastily interpreted it as "only an authorization, not a directive." Meanwhile, from 1945 to 1950, the United States loans to other foreign countries aggregated over thirty-one billions, including nearly seven billions under the Marshall Plan and over 640 millions of special aid to Greece and Turkey.

In October 1950, while Spain continued to be excluded from the North Atlantic Defense Pact, Turkey was admitted to a consultative part in it through an exchange of notes between Mr. Acheson and the Turkish Ambassador in Washington. Our Secretary explained that it was "with regard to the defense of the Mediterranean." Apparently, in his view, the Mediterranean needed defense at only one end.

In November 1950 the United States delegation to the United Nations Assembly did act in accordance with Mr. Acheson's announced "new policy" of the preceding January. In concert with Latin American and other countries, it helped to bring about the repeal of the 1946 resolution and thereby cleared the way for the resumption of full diplomatic relations with Spain. Though President Truman told a press conference on the morrow of the vote that it would be "a long, long time" before he sent an Ambassador to Spain, he took less than two months to name Mr. Stanton Griffis for the post and to welcome Señor Lequerica as regular Spanish Ambassador to this country. In March 1951 Mr. Griffis was received with honor and much popular acclaim in Madrid, and, according to our newspapers, was already in friendly negotiation with General Franco and his Foreign Minister about economic and military ties between Spain and the United States.

Then in July, Admiral Sherman, on behalf of the American Joint Chiefs of Staff and with the approval of President Truman and Secretary Acheson, visited Madrid and discussed with General Franco the possible terms of a special mutual defense pact between the two countries. Spain, it was officially announced, was being asked to grant the United States certain naval and air bases, and the United States stood ready, in return, to supply Spain with military equipment and economic aid.

5.

Such is the strange and curious story of the actual relations between the two countries during the past twelve years. I have dwelt on it at some length because it is so strange and curious—and so twisting. It goes one way from 1939 to 1944, in quite the opposite direction from 1945 to 1949, and now turns back.

There still remains a big undertow of opposition to the resumption and development of friendly coöperation between the two countries. Neither France nor Great Britain is favorable to it. Both of those countries fear lest any aid which we give Spain, financial or military, may lessen our aid to them. Both have been especially fearful of the upsetting effect of any show of friendliness toward "Franco Spain" on their domestic politics—the reaction in Britain of the radical Laborites, and in France of the Socialists as well as the numerous Communists. Both are particularly reluctant to admit Spain to partnership in either the Marshall Plan or the North Atlantic Pact; and our Government, appreciating that they are the chief powers which might help us against Russian aggression, has been understandably reluctant to press policies of which they disapprove. Mr. Acheson has repeatedly intimated that it is up to France and Britain, more than to us, to determine our relationship with Spain.

Within the United States, too, any sort of dictatorship is naturally viewed askance by our democratically minded people, and opposition to "Franco Spain," especially among our Leftist groups, is still a factor in party politics. Moreover, such opposition continues to be fed by partisan and tendentious propaganda, which, if now less heeded than formerly by the masses and by Congress, still exerts enough influence to bolster the anti-Franco attitude of many of our citizens and public officials. In addition to a number of books which have appeared since 1945, advising "toughness" toward the Spanish Government, some of our most widely circulated periodicals have indulged in propaganda of a highly abusive or misleading character. Even some of our most staid and respected journals are not entirely devoid of "slanted" dispatches and editorials about Spain.

Yet despite the continuance of adverse criticism and propaganda, and despite the present timidity or lukewarmness in Britain and France, I venture to predict that the force of circumstances in the world at large will make increasingly for betterment of relations between Spain and the United States.

VII.

Desirable Relations

1.

What is desirable in relations between the United States and Spain should by now be clear. With Spain we should establish and maintain especially close and cordial relations. We should do so in our own interest, in that of the Atlantic Community, and in that of a decent, peaceable world order. And Spain, having like interests, can be counted upon to reciprocate.

There cannot be a peaceful world order and an effective United Nations Organization without a strong and solidified Atlantic Community. There cannot be such a Community without the inclusion of Spain along with her eighteen daughter nations in America. There cannot be first-line defense for the United States without special understanding and coöperation between English-speaking and Spanish-speaking peoples.

The United States is not now the isolated North American power it was sixty years ago, nor even the temporarily balancing power it was in Europe in the First World War of thirty-odd years ago. It is now, in the 1950's, a truly global power, chief of the whole Atlantic Community and predominant throughout the Pacific. The transition has been the result not only of a more or less fortuitous series of foreign wars, from the Spanish-American War through two World Wars, but also of extraordinary domestic developments—a remarkable increase of population and hence of man-power, a still more remarkable attainment of technological, industrial, and financial superiority, and a greatly quickened nationalistic self-consciousness. All this has occurred so recently and rapidly that Americans, as well as foreigners, have had difficulty in adjusting themselves to it and recognizing what logically it entails.

After our decisive participation in the First World War, the idea prevailed among us that a return to isolation would keep us out of a Second. When it didn't, the idea naturally became prevalent that only by abandoning isolation could we escape a Third World War. Yet as a nation we hardly foresaw in 1945, at the close of the Second World War, in what vast global responsibility our abandonment of isolation would involve us. We then saw very dimly, if at all, that the complete disarming of Germany and Japan, combined with the military collapse of France and Italy and the weakened condition of Britain and its Empire, would create a power vacuum between Communist Russia and the United States. Nor did we then imagine how impossible it would be for these two powers to collaborate sincerely and effectually within the organization of the United Nations, or how unbridgeable would be the gulf between their purposes and methods.

We now know better. Sorry experience since 1945 has taught us that Communist Russia is bent on world domination and that it is a far more dangerous threat to our security and way of life than Germany ever was. For the Moscow dictatorship, as a result of its cumulative aggressions, now heads the hugest and potentially richest empire in history—much more extensive than that of an Alexander, a Caesar, or a Genghiz Khan. It is a solid Eurasion land mass, stretching from the China and Yellow Seas to the Baltic and Adriatic, and embracing, with satellites in the Far East and in eastern and central Europe, a population of nearly 800 million, a full third of the estimated total population of the Earth. In contrast, the United States has a population of 150 million, and its present superiority to Russia in mechanical and technological development can only be temporary. And our armed ground forces, compared with those of Communist Russia and China, are pitifully small.

In trying to overcome the discrepancy and at least to "contain" the Communist Empire, we have latterly been rearming and pursuing a threefold foreign policy: (1) maintaining our naval and air predominance in the Pacific and opposing further Communist expansion on its periphery; (2) keeping Russia out of the Mediterranean and Near East; (3), most important, obtaining and strengthening allies that we hope will help us resist Russian aggression in western Europe. The second and third of these policies are obviously interlocked, and in implementing them we have sponsored the Marshall Plan of economic aid and the North Atlantic Pact for defensive military coöperation. Under the Marshall Plan, we have been spending since June 1948 some 20 billion dollars (almost 6 billion for the year 1950) for the rehabilitation of the countries of western and southern Europe —except Spain. By the North Atlantic Pact of April 1949, we have allied with ourselves, and pledged military assistance to, every Atlantic nation in Europe —except Spain; and we have included in it Canada, Iceland, and Italy, and associated with it Turkey and Greece.

We should expand the North Atlantic Pact into a defensive alliance of the whole Atlantic Community, including Spain and Latin America. Spain certainly occupies a strategic geographical position in any plan for the defense of western and southern Europe and of the Atlantic approaches to the American Continents. It is at the gateway through which we have direct contact with the Mediterranean countries of Italy, Greece, Turkey, and Yugoslavia. It also, with Portugal, juts out farther west into the Atlantic than any other European country except Ireland, and is nearest to the Caribbean and South America. It has excellent accessible harbors on both its Atlantic and Mediterranean coasts, and convenient commodious airports in the interior. It can be a bastion for France, and, along with the British Isles, a main depot for us in any war which we may be called upon to wage in Europe.

Spain also has a very considerable man-power of its own, and a man-power which is physically pretty husky and of proven valor. What it lacks is up-to-date military equipment, and a first counsel of wisdom would seem to be for us to help supply that lack. An investment by us in Spain would be surer to strengthen our defense than what we are contributing to certain other countries.

It is important for us to pursue a "good neighbor" policy toward Spain for the sake of maintaining an obviously desirable good neighbor policy toward the eighteen Spanish-speaking republics to the south of us. Spanish America is even more closely linked in culture and sympathy with Spain than is the United States with Britain; and we should not overlook or minimize the fact that the chief opponents of Spain's exclusion from the United Nations, and of other discriminations against her, have been spokesmen of Spanish-American countries. An unfriendly attitude by us toward Spain can alienate from us a third of the American Continents and play into the hands of Communists throughout Spanish America as well as in Europe.

Moreover, Spanish-speaking peoples are in such geographical proximity to Portuguese-speaking peoples alike in the Iberian Peninsula and in South America, and so akin to them in language and culture and nowadays in politics, that at least for strategic purposes they can and should be treated as a unit. Altogether there are some 123 million of them in the world, almost half as many as the number of English-speaking people, and more than the number of Japanese or Germans or French. We have already extended financial aid to Portugal and brought it into defensive alliance with us. We can afford to do no less with Spain. Nor can we afford to lose sight of the desirability of cultivating particularly friendly relations within the *two* triangles of which geographically and historically the United

States is an immediate part: the one triangle of ourselves with Canada and the European mother countries of Britain and France; the other triangle of ourselves with Latin America and the European mother countries of Spain and Portugal. We have not neglected the one. We should not neglect the other.

2.

Collaboration with Spain requires, of course, an overcoming of democratic scruples about General Franco's government, which is undoubtedly a kind of dictatorship—a military and anti-communist dictatorship. Curiously enough, neither we nor the British and French democracies have scrupled too much about other dictatorships. We have done our best for several years to collaborate with Stalin's communist dictatorship. We now bestow favors on Marshal Tito's communist dictatorship in Yugoslavia. We ally ourselves with Portugal which has the same kind of dictatorship as Spain. We are friendly with Latin American governments which have been imposed by military *putsch.* We should not discriminate, in our scruples, against the recognized Spanish Government.

It would be nice, from our standpoint, if General Franco would step aside and be succeeded quite peacefully by an orderly democratic regime similar to ours or to Britain's. That was what our government, jointly with the British and French, requested in 1946. By now, however, it should be clear that General Franco's hold on Spain has actually been strengthened rather than weakened by foreign hostility and ostracism. After all, his government, however much we may regret its military and dictatorial character, does represent that part of the Spanish nation which won a desperate three-year civil war; and it would indeed be quite a novelty in human history if the victors in such a war, at the behest of foreigners, should say to the vanquished only a few years afterwards: "We are sorry, we shouldn't have won the war; we're now turning over the government to you!" Imagine, a few years after our own Civil War, General Grant saying that to the Confederates, and imagine what the effect would have been if Tsarist Russia, with England and France, had told him to say it!

Besides, what would be the alternative to the present regime in Spain? Most Spaniards, including many who heartily dislike Franco and are highly critical of his rule, fear the alternative would be a renewal of domestic strife between "Leftists" and "Rightists," Republicans and Monarchists, Liberals and Traditionalists, Anarchists and Socialists, and a consequent recurrence of violence and civil war, ending in another kind of dictatorship worse than the present. To some, it would seem like "jumping from the frying pan into the fire."

This attitude goes far to explain why the constitutional monarchy has not been restored in Spain, as Don Juan, the son of Alfonso XIII, repeatedly urges. Certainly there are many avowed Spanish royalists, especially among the upper and middle classes. But while they criticize General Franco and hope for his voluntary retirement, they rely upon him to keep order and are fearful of the revolutionary consequences of any forcible attempt to supplant him with Don Juan. Which is as understandable to Spaniards as it is disappointing to foreigners. I recall with what sadness my British colleague in Madrid told me he knew of no other country where there were so many monarchists who really didn't want a king. When he asked me what I thought about Spain's political future, I said I simply didn't know. The problem was, and is, too complex for me. If it can be solved at all, only Spaniards can do it, and time and patience are required.

At any rate, we should bear in mind that the existing Spanish Government is not a totalitarian dictatorship of the same sort as Hitler's or Stalin's. For the essence of totalitarianism is its deification of the "total state," its determination to remold the individual into a creature of the state. It has no room for religion, capitalist initiative, or any other personal interests and allegiance. And it is always dynamic, expanding, and fanatically proselyting—a movement to be imposed upon other peoples by propaganda and force. Into this totalitarian pattern the Spanish regime of General Franco, whatever its faults and shortcomings, simply does not fit. On the contrary, in the words of a popular American journal, "it clings to old institutions and traditions, notably the church, instead of trying to replace them. It is not strongly ideological. It does not propagandize itself as the utopian answer to everything, or as an irresistible urge of historical force. Franco himself calls his government 'provisional' and speaks of a future return to 'normalization.' "[1]

Franco has repeatedly declared that his military dictatorship is temporary, and during the past nine years he has taken steps to moderate it and to transform it into a constitutional regime. A national Cortes, similar to Portugal's, has been functioning since 1942. A system of local administration and elections was inaugurated in 1944. A charter of individual liberties was issued in 1945. The number of political prisoners has steadily declined. The Falange organization has been restricted. Censorship of the press has been eased. In 1947 a popular plebiscite endorsed, by a

[1] *Time*, December 20, 1948.

large majority, a "succession law," providing for a possible eventual restoration of the monarchy and for the establishment of a Council of Regency to nominate Franco's successor in case of his death, resignation, or incapacity.

This liberalizing transition of the Spanish Government was in process *before* the United States joined Russia in denouncing General Franco and prevailing upon the United Nations to ostracize Spain; and there is reason to believe that, had it not been for this unfortunate and mistaken action, the political transition within Spain would have proceeded faster. There is now, as there was then, a much greater chance of speeding the process through friendly counsel and example than through employment of abuse and threats and boycotts.

My own conviction—and in this I merely express what until rather recently has been a tradition and practice of the United States—is that we should not concern ourselves with the internal affairs or form of government of any foreign country, unless that country becomes, or clearly threatens to become, a menace to the peace and independence of its neighbors and hence of the world and of ourselves. This was the time-honored policy which the founding fathers of our Republic enunciated and which President Franklin Roosevelt reaffirmed in specific pledges to Spain in

1942. It should not have been repudiated in 1945–1946, and it should now be fully reinstated and strictly adhered to.

Quite aside from any question of expediency or of favor we may hope to obtain, it is extremely important and vitally necessary that we observe a high standard of morality in our dealings with foreign countries. As an avowed upholder of public morality against a notoriously cynical Hitler or Stalin, we must not allow our Government to be deceitful or hypocritical, as I fear it has been during the last few years about Spain. To Spain, our President gave solemn promises in 1942 which we went back on in 1946. Justice and ordinary decency require that we retrace our steps and respect those promises. There is certainly nothing in the attitude of Spain or of its government toward us which can honestly justify any other course. During the World War, it granted more favors to us, and likewise to Britain and France, than did such other neutrals as Turkey, Switzerland, or Sweden. And now, assuredly, it is no menace to peace, but rather a potential contributor to the defense of its European neighbors and ourselves.

It is frequently alleged that Spain is a greater concern of its European neighbors, France and Great Britain, than of the United States, and that therefore our attitude toward it should be determined by theirs.

There is no doubt that both those countries are especially concerned for reasons of domestic politics. The Labor party in Britain and still more the Socialists and Radicals in France not only are opposed on "Leftist" democratic principles to the "Rightist" dictatorship in Spain, but are fearful lest any collaboration with it will cost them electoral support at home and redound to the advantage of the extremists and communists in their midst. In France, we should remember, the number of Communists, though lately declining, is still dangerously large.

We rightfully regard France and Britain as our major allies in the defense of western Europe against Russian and Communist aggression. Yet it would seem very unfortunate if, through tenderness toward partisan extremists, they should induce us to neglect any possible means of strengthening and adding to that defense. Fundamentally it is as much to the interest of France and Britain as to ours that Spain, no less than Portugal, should be treated as part and parcel of the Atlantic Community, and I for one believe that realistic statesmanship at Washington could so convince the politicians at Paris and London. In this we should be leaders, rather than mere followers, for Spain's strategic position and its cultural ties with so much of the American continents make it a direct concern of the United States.

3.

Proper and desirable relations between the United States and Spain will hardly be achieved unless, below the government level, the people of the two countries acquire a sounder knowledge of each other than they possess today. Ignorance and prejudice exist in Spain about life and thought in the United States. Most Spaniards are apt to judge Americans by the meretricious Hollywood films they see or the boastful advertising radio broadcasts they hear from New York and to conclude that we are crass materialists or uncultured barbarians. They envy our machinery and motor cars and gadgets, but they are suspicious of our motives and fearful of our power. They perceive in us a "holier-than-thou" attitude which they interpret as hypocrisy.

Popular ignorance and prejudice in the United States about Spain can only be described as colossal. Few Americans are willing or able to view Spaniards at all realistically, and to recognize in them virtues as well as faults. The minority among us who try to sympathize with Spain are likely to be pretty romantic about it. The large majority are apparently content to fall back on the old stereotypes and slogans about Spanish intolerance, cruelty, and backwardness.

We must have in both countries an increasing number of influential persons—educators, publicists, clergymen, literary and business men—who will interest themselves in counteracting current mythical notions and obtaining and spreading in the one country sympathetic solid information about the other. We in the United States should have more Spanish history in our colleges, more traveling in Spain, more appreciation of Spanish literature and art. On the other hand, Spaniards should have more United States history in their universities, more traveling here, better understanding of our idealism.

Spain greatly needs political stability, with orderly progress toward free democracy. For this it can learn much from the United States as well as from restudy and revival of its own medieval and early modern traditions. But it is not going to have political stability and better government so long as the United States, in concert with certain other countries, treats Spain as a social pariah and seeks to starve the Spanish people into revolt. If anywhere the cause of stable democratic government is served, not by starvation, but by economic betterment of the masses, it should be so in Spain. For such betterment, Spain needs both industrial and agricultural development. It has particular need of hydro-electric and other machinery and of the technology which we can and should help to supply.

It likewise needs a lowering of our tariff barriers against its exports. Incidentally we might bear in mind that Spaniards, even under adverse circumstances, have an excellent record of paying their foreign debts.

A special and earnest effort should be made to overcome the religious prejudice which has too long and too heavily beclouded relations between English-speaking and Spanish-speaking peoples. Closer contact between leading Catholic clergy and laymen of Spain and those of the United States should broaden the viewpoints of both. American Protestants would be more convincing exponents of religious tolerance and freedom if they had a better knowledge of Catholicism and were less intolerant of its expression in Spain. Irreligion exists in Spain as well as in the United States, and it troubles Catholics there as it here troubles Protestants and Catholics and Jews. The unbelievers and irreligious of both countries have little difficulty in understanding each other and on occasion in coöperating. Christian charity should make possible similar mutual understanding and coöperation among religious believers of both.

Cultural differences do exist between the United States and Spain. They derive from differences of habitat and history, and they will doubtless continue into a distant future. Hence it is needful not only that the two peoples learn more about each other but that they learn to respect their differences.

Yet the fact of cultural difference should not obscure the still more significant fact that both peoples share a common basic civilization. Spain and the United States alike are "Western" nations, heirs of Greece and Rome, and partners in the European-American Atlantic Community. What harms one in this partnership harms the other. What helps one helps the other. Nor is it a matter just between the United States and Spain. The United States has special ties with Canada and Great Britain. Spain has special ties with Portugal and Latin America. The two groups, English-speaking and Hispanic-speaking, by working together can provide the keystone for a solid trans-Atlantic bridge, the cement of the whole Atlantic Community, and a surety of world peace.

Select Bibliography

1. General Description and Characterization of Spain

On Spanish traits: Salvador de Madariaga, *Englishmen, Frenchmen, Spaniards* (1928), and *Spain* (1942); José Ortega y Gasset, *Invertebrate Spain* (1937); Havelock Ellis, *The Soul of Spain* (1929); Louis Bertrand, *Espagne* (1934).

Important travel books: Georgia Long, *All about Spain* (1951); Sacheverell Sitwell, *Spain* (1950).

On the Catalans: E. Allison Peers, *Catalonia Infelix* (1937); Anton Sieberer, *Katalonien gegen Kastilien* (1936).

On the Basques: Julio Caro Baroja, *Los vascos* (1950), anthropological and historical; José Antonio de Aguirre, *Escape via Berlin* (1944), containing, in its last part, a presentation of Basque nationalism, by the Basque President during the Spanish Civil War.

2. Background of Spanish History

The most detailed, scholarly, and up-to-date general history of Spain is the twelve-volume work of Antonio Ballesteros y Beretta, *Historia de España y de su influencia en la historia universal,* 2nd ed. (1943–1948), which unfortunately has not been translated into English. It supersedes the classic "liberal" work of Rafael Altamira y Crevea, *Historia de España y de la civilización española,* 3rd ed., 4 vols (1913–1914), parts of which have been translated into English by Charles E. Chapman (1935) and Muna Lee (1949). There is a brilliant volume by Ramón Menéndez Pidal, *The Spaniards in their History*, translated with a fine introduction by Walter Starkie (1950). There is also an English translation by Aubrey G. F. Bell of the *History of Iberian Civilization* (1930) by the famous Portuguese historian, Joaquim Pedro Oliveira Martins, covering both Spain and Portugal. The best brief summary is H. D. Sedgwick, *Spain, a Short History* (1925).

On Spanish literature: James Fitzmaurice-Kelly, *New History of Spanish Literature* (1926); Angel del Rio, *Historia de la literatura española* (1948).

On special periods: Roger B. Merriman, *Rise of the Spanish Empire in the Old World and in the New,* 4 vols (1918–1930), to death of Philip II; Earl J. Hamilton, *American Treasure and the Price Revolution in Spain* (1934), economics in the 16th and 17th centuries; François Rousseau, *Règne de Charles III d'Espagne, 1759–1788*, 2 vols (1907), on the "Enlightenment" and French influence in Spain; Robert Sencourt, *Spain's Uncertain Crown, the Story of Spanish Sovereigns 1808–1931* (1932); Francisco Pi y Margall & Francisco Pi y Arsuaga, *Los grandes conmociones políticos del siglo XIX en España,* 2 vols (1933); Conde de Romanones, *Las responsibilidades políticas del antiquo régimen de 1875 a 1923* (1924), and *Los últimas horas de una monarquía* (1931); Duque de Maura & Melchor Fernández Almagro, *Porqué cayó Alfonso XIII, Evolución y disolución de los partidos históricos durante su reinado,* 2nd ed. (1948).

3. Spain in America and United States Foreign Policy

On Spanish America: C. H. Haring, *The Spanish Empire in America* (1947); Salvador de Madariaga, *The Rise and The Fall of the Spanish American Empire*, 2 vols (1947); J. F. Rippy, *Historical Evolution of Hispanic America*, 2nd ed. (1940); Frank Tannenbaum, *Slave or Citizen* (1947).

On United States Foreign Policy: Samuel Flagg Bemis, *The Latin American Policy of the United States* (1943) and *Diplomatic History of the United States*, 3rd ed. (1950); Thomas A. Bailey, *A Diplomatic History of the American People*, 4th ed. (1950); Dexter Perkins, *Hands Off, a History of the Monroe Doctrine* (1941); Arthur P. Whitaker, *The United States and the Independence of Latin America, 1800–1830* (1941); Walter Millis, *The Martial Spirit* (1931), on the Spanish-American War of 1898; Gregory Mason, *Remember the Maine* (1939).

4. Church, Land, Army, and Political Doctrine in Spain

On the Church: E. Allison Peers, *Spain, the Church and the Orders* (1945), excellent survey of developments since 1700; José Maria Doussinague, *Hispanidad y catolicismo* (1939); Severino Aznar, *El catolicismo social en España* (1906) and *Estudios económico-sociales* (1946), on Catholic social action.

On land questions: Pascual Carrión, *Los latifundios en España* (1932), account of land holdings and distribution; Gerald Brenan, *The Spanish Labyrinth* (1943), especially good on agriculture and the peasantry in different parts of the country.

On the army as a political force: Conde de Romanones, *El ejército y la política* (1920).

On liberalism and freemasonry: Luis Diez del Corral, *El liberalismo doctrinario* (1948); Rhea Marsh Smith, *The Day of the Liberals in Spain* (1938); Marcelino Menéndez y Pelayo, *Historia de los heterodoxos españoles*, 2nd ed., 7 vols (1911–1932); Vicente de la Fuente, *Historia de las sociedades seeretas y modernas en España y especialmente de la francmasonería*, new ed., 3 vols (1933).

On traditionalism: Ramiro de Maeztu, *Defensa de la Hispanidad*, 5th ed. (1946).

On socialism and anarchism: Juan José Morato, *El partido socialista* (1931); Gerald Brenan, *The Spanish Labyrinth* (1943).

5. The Republic and Civil War, 1931–1939

E. Allison Peers, *The Spanish Tragedy, 1930–1936, Dictatorship, Republic, Chaos*, 3rd ed. (1936), best single account of the Republic; Melchor Fernández Almagro, *Historia de la república española, 1931–1936* (1940); José Pla, *Historia de la segunda república española*, 4 vols (1940), with documents; Richard Pattee, *This is Spain* (1951), pro-Nationalist, with historical background and full bibliography; Arthur Loveday, *Spain 1923–1948* (1949), summary by an English business man resident in Spain; Alejandro Lerroux, *Al servicio de la república* (1930) and *La pequeña historia* (1945), by the Moderate Republican leader.

Franz Borkenau, *The Spanish Cockpit* (1937), and *The Communist International* (1939) with a short chapter on Spanish Communists; Enrique Castro Delgado, *J'ai perdu la foi à Moscou*, 11th ed. (1950), by former official delegate of the Spanish Communist party to the Comintern; Julian Zugazagoitía, *Historia de la guerra en España*, by member of the Republican Government.

Strongly "Leftist" accounts: Julio Alvarez del Vayo, *Freedom's Battle* (1940); Ernest Hemingway, *The Spanish War* (1938); Constancia de la Mora, *In Place of Splendour* (1940).

"Rightist" accounts: H. Edward Knoblaugh, *Correspondent in Spain* (1937); Arnold Lunn, *Spanish Rehearsal* (1937); Robert Sencourt, *Spain's Ordeal* (1938); Kate O'Brien, *Farewell to Spain* (1937).

A pro-Republican Catholic view is supplied by Alfred Mendizábal, *The Martyrdom of Spain*, with an Introduction by Jacques Maritain (1938).

On German-Spanish relations during the Civil War: *Documents on German Foreign Policy*, Series D, Vol. III (1950).

6. *Spain during World War II and After*

On foreign relations and diplomacy: E. Allison Peers, *Spain in Eclipse, 1937–1943*, 2nd ed. (1945); Dwight D. Eisenhower, *Crusade in Europe* (1948); Carlton J. H. Hayes, *Wartime Mission in Spain 1942–1945* (1945), account of American Ambassador at Madrid; Sir Samuel Hoare (Viscount Templewood), *Complacent Dictator* (1947), account of British Ambassador; José Maria de Areilza, *Embajadores sobre España*, 3rd ed. (1947), Spanish commentary on accounts of Hayes and Hoare; Ramón Serrano Suñer, *Entre Hendaya y Gibraltar* (1947), apology of the pro-Axis Spanish Foreign Minister who was retired in 1942; José Maria Doussinague, *España tenía razón 1939–1945*, 2nd ed. (1950), a somewhat naive and gullible defense of Spanish foreign policy; Herbert Feis, *The Spanish Story, Franco and the Nations at War* (1948), a partial and limited view of an official of the U. S. State Department who differed from some of his colleagues about American policy toward

Spain; Department of State, *The Spanish Government and the Axis* (1946), a tendentious "white paper"; W. L. Beaulac, *Career Ambassador* (1951), illuminating memoirs of a foreign service officer who was Counselor of the American Embassy in Madrid from 1941 to 1944.

Anti-Franco criticism and propaganda: Thomas J. Hamilton, *Appeasement's Child, the Franco Regime in Spain* (1943); Allan Chase, *Falange, the Axis Secret Enemy in the Americas* (1943); The "Nation" Associates, *The Case for Action against Franco and the Recognition of the Spanish Republic by the United Nations* (1946); Emmet John Hughes, *Report from Spain* (1947); Charles Foltz, *The Masquerade in Spain* (1948).

In behalf of the Franco Regime: Richard Pattee, *This is Spain* (1951); Arthur Loveday, *Spain* (1948).